MW00986231

The Seven Points
of Mind Training

The Seven Points of Mind Training

by

THE VENERABLE
KHENCHEN THRANGU RINPOCHE

translated by
Maruta Stern & Erik Pema Kunsang

root text translated by
Michele Martin

edited by
Victoria Huckenpahler

Zhyisil Chokyi Ghatsal Charitable Trust
Publications

Acknowledgment

We would like to express our sincere thanks and appreciation to Khenchen Thrangu Rinpoche for his great compassion and wisdom in bestowing these precious teachings.

We would also like to thank the many persons who helped make this book possible. First, we would like to thank Maruta Stern for translating the teachings given in Nepal, Erik Kunsang for translating the teaching given in Maine, and Michele Martin for translating the root text and for rendering extensive editing assistance. We would also thank Gaby Hollmann for transcribing and helping to edit the tapes of the retreat. And especially Ckark and Pat Johnson for their tireless work in preserving and making available the teachings of Khenchen Thrangu Rinpoche.

This book is dedicated to:

His Holiness, the 17th Gyalwa Karmapa,
Urgen Trinley Dorje.
May he live long and prosper and spread the true
Dharma throughout the world.

Copyright © 2004 by Thrangu Rinpoche.
Root text © 2004 Michele Martin

All rights reserved. No part of this book, either text or art, may be reproduced in any form, electronic or otherwise, without written permission from the Namo Buddha Seminar or Thrangu Rinpoche.

Published by Namo Buddha Publications
P. O. Box 1083, Crestone, CO 81131
Tel.: (719) 256-5539
E-mail: cjohnson@ix.netcom.com
Web site: www.NamoBuddhaPub.org
and
Zhyisil Chokyi Ghatsal Publications
P.O. Box 6259, Wellesley St, Auckland, NZ
Tel.: (649) 268 0786
Email: inquiries@greatliberation.org
Web site. www.greatliberation.org

National Library of New Zealand Cataloguing-in-Publication Data

Thrangu, Rinpoche, 1933-
The seven points of mind training / by Khabje Thrangu Rinpoche;
translated by Maruta Stern and Erik Pema Kunsang; root text
translated by Michele Martin; edited by Victoria Huckenpahler.
Includes bibliographical references and index.
ISBN 1-877294-37-3
1. Blo-sbyon. 2. Meditation—Buddhism. I. Huckenpahler,
Victoria, 1945- II. Zhyisil Chokyi Ghatsal Trust. III. Title.
294.34435—dc 22

Note

Words are given as they are pronounced, not as they are spelled. The actual spellings of Tibetan words are given in the Glossary of Tibetan Terms.

We use the convention of B.C.E. (Before Current Era) for what is known as B.C. and C.E. (Current Era) for A.D.

These teachings were given in Nepal at the Namo Buddha Seminar in January, 1993 in Nepal and in Maine, USA in September of 2001.

TABLE OF CONTENTS

VENERABLE CHOJE LAMA SHEDRUP

Foreword

THE ESSENCE OF ALL THE TEACHINGS taught by the Lord Buddha concern taming one's mind, the point being to return the mind to its natural state of freedom which is endowed with limitless qualities. The realization of this natural state gives rise to spontaneous compassion that is limitless and impartial. This is "awakening mind" or "ultimate bodhichitta." In order to develop and realize this we engage in the supreme path of cultivating great loving kindness and compassion – relative bodhichitta. This is the very foundation and essence of the Mahayana and Vajrayana.

The Seven Points of Mind Training, compiled in pithy points and slogans, is one of the most well known, profound and traditional practices and text's to develop bodhichitta. Dipamkara Srijana (Atisha), the founder of the Kadampa tradition, originally received this as a transmission from his supreme master Dharmakirti. Atisha brought this great transmission lineage to Tibet, and *The Seven Points of Mind Training* teachings have since been assimilated by all the Tibetan Buddhist schools. This precious practice lineage has been kept alive as a pure and continuous stream of blessing from the Buddha, passed from teacher to disciple, until the present.

Yet in order to fully convey the profound and rich meaning of these pithy slogans, what is required and of most benefit is a contemporary teacher who has himself realized and embodies bodhichitta. Such a sublime master is Khabje Khenchen Thrangu

Rinpoche, who with great compassion, clarity and simplicity illuminates the profound meaning and methods of these teachings so they can become a part of our daily life and practice.

May this publication be a cause for the life and teachings of the great masters to flourish and remain for many eons bringing all beings to awakening.

Kagyu Thigsum Chokyi Ghatsal
Tibetan Buddhist Centre
Launceston, Tasmania, Australia
May 2006

PREFACE

TIBET WAS NON-BUDDHIST UNTIL the eighth century when its King, Trisong Deutsen, asked Padmasambhava to come to Tibet to introduce the Buddhist teachings there. It was Padmasambhava, along with the Indian scholar Shantarakshita, who established Samye Monastery in 779 C.E. To help in this endeavor, the Minister Thonmi Sambhota was sent to India to develop a written script for the Tibetans. Thereafter, numerous Tibetans made perilous journeys to India to bring back the dharma and translate it into Tibetan.

This text on mind training, called *lojong* in Tibetan, was brought to Tibet by Atisha in the eleventh century. Atisha brought over 100 instructions to Tibet, this particular text being compiled by one of his students who condensed it into the present form of seven points.

The Buddhism of Tibet was a combination of the Shravakayana, Mahayana, and Vajrayana. The Shravakayana sometimes called the Hinayana was practiced in terms of strict personal discipline and the fundamental meditation of Shamatha and Vipashyana. The Mahayana was taught in terms of engaging in an extensive study of the emptiness doctrine of the Middle Way (Skt. *Madhyamaka*) school and taking the Mahayana vow to help all living beings reach liberation. Helping all beings was accomplished through the practice of the six perfections (Skt. *paramitas*) (generosity, morality, patience, perseverance, meditative stabilization, and wisdom). The Vajrayana was achieved through yidam practices and the practice of examining mind directly, using Dzogchen or Mahamudra meditation.

The study of texts on the Middle Way concerning emptiness took a minimum of a year in the monastic college or *shedra* which, unlike our colleges, involved an eight to ten hour daily study, six to seven days a week, with only a few weeks of vacation a year. The study of the Middle Way was achieved by memorizing the root texts in the morning, then receiving a commentary such as Thrangu Rinpoche has provided in this book in the late morning, and then debating the points of the text in the afternoon. Sometimes these texts were studied not just conceptually, but in conjunction with analytical meditation. At Rumtek monastery in the Nalanda Shedra, for example, Khenpo Tsultrim Rinpoche would teach emptiness in the morning, and in the afternoon would have the students face the outside walls and go into a deep meditation while he would read passages from the sutras on these topics.

Another method for actually practicing the Mahayana is Atisha's mind training practice. The purpose of this practice is to overcome the habitual tendency to center the world around ourselves, and thus decrease our ego. The belief in "I" and in what we hold as "mine" causes vast amounts of harm in the world. This habit of acting in terms of "self" and "other" comes from placing ourselves over others in terms of our nation, our race, our community and social class, right down to believing that we are somehow fundamentally better than friends and even family members.

When asked whether he felt anger towards the Chinese for surrounding his camp with machine guns when he was fleeing Tibet in 1959, opening fire on him and hundreds of others, Thrangu Rinpoche replied "No," because the soldiers were doing what they were supposed to do—shoot at him—and he was doing what he was supposed to do—run for his life.

To reverse this belief in holding our body and our ideas to be extremely important, we must put others ahead of our own selfish, ego-clinging patterns. The *Seven Points of Mind Training* constitute exactly such a practice, beginning the second we wake up and then carrying the attitude on through-out the day as we eat, work, and socialize with others. Practice ends at night when we examine ourselves to see if we have followed the mind training principles. Finally, Thrangu Rinpoche has suggested that as we fall asleep we should do sending and taking practice.

Mind training is relevant for modern times because we do not need to go to an isolated cave or retreat to engage in it; we can engage in it while doing all the thousands of other things we do every day. This practice has also been condensed to a few dozen instructions which are easy to memorize, and which are actually standards for living our daily life. They tell us how to behave in ordinary circumstances and show us if our ego is increasing or decreasing. In modern life, we do not usually have the time or patience to memorize long texts, so this practice is perfectly adopted for the present day.

These teachings on the *Seven Points of Mind Training* were given on two different occasions: in 1993 with Maruta Stern translating and also in 2001 in Maine with Erik Kunsang translating. Since Rinpoche emphasized certain points in one teaching and other points in others, we have combined the two.

Clark Johnson, Ph.D.
Managing Editor
Namo Buddha Publications

DIPAMKARA SRIJANA

The Bodhisattva Atisha

chapter one

AN INTRODUCTION TO MIND TRAINING

Why We Should Study Mind Training

IN THE PREVIOUS YEARS, I TAUGHT the general approach of Buddhist practice and I have also given the instructions on the Shamatha and Vipashyana meditation according to Mahamudra. These teachings are very pithy and profound and they are especially aimed at achieving the ultimate level of reality. There is, however, a way of practice that places more emphasis on the relative or the conventional level of reality. Some of my students have asked, "I practice Mahamudra and it is very beneficial, but every so often strong disturbing emotions well up and the Mahamudra practice doesn't seem to stop them. What should I do then?" This is a good question to ask because at such times there is a way of practice that emphasizes more the relative truth and this is a teaching known as *The Seven Points of Mind Training*, which is very useful because it can help us pacify the emotions.

This is not just my personal opinion. The Seven Points have been practiced by the lineage of masters up to the present. They are explained as the merging of two rivers, the Kadampa and Mahamudra instructions, into one style of practice. Gampopa fused the mind training instructions of the Kadampa together with the Mahamudra instructions which he received from the great master Milarepa. In this way, there has been a line of practitioners known as "the golden rosary" or "chain of golden links" which has remained unbroken until the present time. This tradition combines mind training together with the profound instructions of Mahamudra. I consider this long tradition as a very important and a very profound approach.

The Story of Atisha

The teachings on *The Seven Points of Mind Training* are regarded as contemplations. They were condensed from the words of the Buddha (Skt. *sutras*) or the treatises (Skt. *shastras*) by the Indian master Atisha.[1] When he first embarked in the dharma, he understood that the attainment of full and complete enlightenment depends upon forming both relative and ultimate or absolute bodhichitta. Since he wanted to find out which is the way to make sure that the true bodhichitta dawns within individuals, he fervently prayed to the deity Tara. He had several visions of her; in one vision Tara made the prediction that Atisha should set out to meet three important masters to receive the transmission of how to be a true bodhisattva and develop the bodhichitta attitude. These three masters were Jampey Naljor, Dharma Rakshita,[2] and Jowo Serlingpa, the Guru from Serling. Of these three, Dharma Rakshita had an incredible life story and exemplified the bodhisattva ideal perfectly. It is said that he even gave away parts of his own flesh to someone who was needy. Atisha's other guru was called Jampey Naljor meaning "the yogi of loving-kindness," because he had that quality of bodhichitta. But the most important of these three was Jowo Serlingpa.

Atisha was born in the present district of Bengal but he went to Nalanda University to study. While studying at Nalanda he heard about Serlingpa. Serling is the Tibetan name for the island of Sumatra and his name means "the master from Sumatra." In those days the Buddhadharma had spread to Indonesia and there were a great number of ordained monks studying with Serlingpa. He was so well-known that his fame had spread all the way to Nalanda in Northern India. When Atisha heard about Jowo Serlingpa, he made up his mind to go and visit. In those days this was a very difficult journey to undertake. Atisha almost died on the way because of violent storms, but whenever obstacles arose, he made fervent prayers to his chief deity Tara and always practiced loving-kindness and compassion. He somehow arrived and was accepted by Serlingpa, who told him, "Yes, bodhichitta is the most important practice and you must practice mind training. But don't think you can do it in just a few days. It takes a long time to perfect this practice. You should stay here until you have completed this training." So Atisha stayed with Serlingpa for twelve years and at the end of that time he had perfected his practice of mind training and returned to India.

Atisha became a great teacher at Nalanda University in Northern India and finally went to Tibet. In the eighth century C.E. Padmasambhava and Shantarakshita had gone to Tibet and established very pure Buddhist teachings. It had been a perfect time to establish Buddhism in Tibet, and the dharma flourished. In the following century, Tibet fell under the influence of King Langdarma who almost obliterated the Buddhist teachings, the lineage of precepts, and its institutions.

Following Langdarma's assassination in 808 C.E., many teachers emerged and some taught their own dharma by, for example, mixing Buddhist practices with black magic. In one of the districts in western Tibet, there was a king called Yeshe Ö ("wisdom light"), who wanted to determine what the true dharma was and what distortions of the Buddhist teachings were so he invited genuine Buddhist teachers to come to Tibet. After him, his successor Jangchub Ö, ("the light of enlightenment"), had the same intention, and he also invited Buddhist teachers to Tibet.

King Yeshe Ö sent numerous translators to India in order to achieve this aim and many of them died on the way. But a few who succeeded in reaching Atisha gave him the king's request. Atisha replied, "It is not a matter of personal feelings of going or not going. I will make supplications to my yidam deity and will wait for the reply." So, he made many supplications to Tara, asking, "Will it be worthwhile for me to go to Tibet?" Tara appeared to him and said, "If you go to Tibet, it will insure that the Buddhadharma again becomes reestablished in that country, but it will also shorten your own life by ten years." Atisha replied, "If I live ten years less, it doesn't matter because what concerns me the most is that the Buddhadharma help living beings. That's what my life is meant for. So, I will go." When Atisha arrived in Tibet, he started from the very beginning by teaching about refuge, bodhichitta, and mind training to separate the true teachings from the distortions. Atisha went to Tibet in 1044 C.E. and remained there until the end of his life.

Atisha founded the Kadampa lineage and when he passed on, he left behind three outstanding disciples, the main one being Drom Tonpa Gyalwai Jungnae. In general, the Kadampa teachings were divided into three sections. One is the Kadampa philosophical texts, which were held by the Riwo Gendunpa or the Gelugpa tradition. Another is the Kadampa secret oral instructions which were held by Dakpo Lhaje (Gampopa) of the Kagyu tradition. The final one is the key instructions of the sixteen spheres which are practiced by everyone. Of these three, we practice the oral instructions which have passed from Gampopa down to this present time.

Gampopa, prior to meeting Milarepa, had followed the Kadampa teachings and received instructions from that lineage. When he was about to meet Milarepa, Milarepa told his disciples, "Today there will come a true teacher from the Kadampa tradition. Whoever escorts him into my presence will never be reborn into the three lower realms." Milarepa understood Gampopa's value from the very start. Also, when Gampopa was leaving after having received all the teachings on Mahamudra, the Six Yogas of Naropa, and so forth, Milarepa escorted him to Garjeling in Gampo where Gampopa began to practice. At this time Milarepa told him that he had had a special dream: from his side a vulture flew forth and landed on the Lhachi Mountain Peak and became surrounded by numerous golden geese, each of which was surrounded by 500 more geese. When they all flew high, the whole area turned a golden color. Milarepa said, "Even though I am a follower of the yogi tradition, an eminent disciple of mine will fuse the Kadampa and Mahamudra lineage."

The teachings on mind training have been articulated in various ways. There is one set of teachings called *Eight Verses for Training the Mind* and another called *Mind Training like a Peacock Overcoming Poison*. There are many other instructions like these. The one that is most popular is known as *The Seven Points of Mind Training*, which is what we will actually practice after having received instructions. *The Seven Points of Mind Training* was written by a master called Chekawa Yeshe Dorje,[3] who went through many difficulties to receive these teachings.

The Bodhisattva Vow

The bodhisattva vow constitutes a major part of the Mahayana path. One of the main ways to accomplish this vow is through the practice of mind training. This mind training, or *lojong* in Tibetan, that we are studying is composed of seven precepts whose purpose is to develop a feeling of love, compassion, and bodhichitta for all living beings. Usually, we tend to think of ourselves as really important. If we have any kind of suffering, we think that it is unbearable and that nobody else suffers as we do. We want to have happiness for ourselves and do not really consider that others feel the same. But the foundation for love, compassion, and bodhichitta is to think that others are equal to us and that we are able to exchange ourselves for them. Actually to do this we have to rid ourselves of this notion that only we are important, that only our suffering is unbearable, and that our desire for joy is of paramount importance. How do we train our mind to do this? The first step is to realize: "If I feel that I am important and that my suffering is unbearable, then other beings must have the same attitude. When they suffer, they too must feel that this suffering is "unbearable." This is the meaning of training the mind.

We may ask how Mahamudra meditation and mind training are related. There are two kinds of truths, conventional and ultimate. Mahamudra is a very high level teaching which concerns the ultimate truth. But sometimes we are unable to realize that ultimate meaning, and because of this, various things happen. Sometimes our meditation goes very well, but at other times our diligence decreases, our pride increases, and our meditation doesn't work the way it should. During these down times, the instructions of mind training are very good. Often people come to me and say: "I really want to practice dharma. I really want to study. I want to meditate but it seems I am very lazy and cannot do it." For times like this, it is very helpful to contemplate again and again the instructions of mind training. In fact, if we can do this over and over, then the diligence which has decreased will again increase, as will faith. This is what the mind training precepts are for: the times when these obstacles, called "inner obstacles of the mind," occur. When this happens, contemplate these thoughts over and over again. When diligence is decreasing and pride and jealousy are increasing, all of the mind instructions help. Once we have contemplated them repeatedly, then we can again go back to Mahamudra practice.

Atisha formulated about a hundred different mind training instructions. In *Advice from a Spiritual Friend* it states that Geshe Chekawa, who inherited the teachings from a disciple of one of Atisha's disciples, put these instructions into the form of the seven points of mind training.

The first part of the mind training is a presentation of the preliminaries, which are the bases for dharma practice. In this text, the preliminaries are divided into two parts: the contemplation at the beginning of the preliminaries, i.e., what we must visualize and think of when we start, and then the actual explanation of the preliminaries.

Questions

Question: Is there a relationship between this practice and *The Wheel of Sharp Weapons*.

Rinpoche: This text and *The Wheel of Sharp Weapons* are basically the same instructions, but are a little different in the meditation instructions. Both are very powerful, as the title suggests, really forceful in getting rid of negativities.

Question: Do the inner obstacles arise because of past bad karma? Could inner obstacles be purified through purification practice?

Rinpoche: Inner obstacles do not come from previous karma. What comes from previous karma are such things as physical suffering and being born in poverty. Inner obstacles, which are various negative conceptual thoughts, come from previous negative habits of thinking. What does purify inner obstacles is, for instance, contemplation on the four thoughts which turn the mind, because inner obstacles are very, very old habits. Doing the four contemplations will gradually change the negative habits of mind and that will clear away the inner obstacles.

Question: When anything happens, negative or positive, to what extent does this depend on karma? For instance, if I am in a train accident, it is my karma, or could it also be the bad repair of the train? Or if something positive happens, like I find money and am happy, is that due simply to the fact that somebody lost this money?

Rinpoche: Not everything is karma. There are two things to consider: your previous karma and the immediate circumstances. Things like our physical suffering, or whether we are wealthy or impoverished, depend upon previous karma. Other things, like our state of mind, are more dependent upon circumstances than upon karma. For instance, if we have good dharma friends with us, then it might be that our mind is in a good place for practicing and we are quite happy most of the time, whereas when we are around people who are not good for us, then our state of mind will not be good either, so we will be quick to become angry. That is called "the circumstance." It functions more like *barche*, which could sometimes be an accident and sometimes a misfortune of some kind. It is based more upon immediate circumstances than upon karma. An airplane accident is karma, the karma of all the victims coming together at one time. It was their karma that they had all gathered together in that airplane. Another example: a man in India wants to get on the bus but doesn't have one rupee, so he can't get on. The bus crashes and everybody dies. It was his karma not to get on that bus, based upon the fact that he didn't have that one rupee. That was his karma.

Question: It is very difficult to distinguish between circumstances and karma. For instance, if a brick drops on my head or my lama passes away, is it my karma or is it also his karma to pass away?

Rinpoche: If a rock falls on your head, it is karma. If it just falls from nowhere and you didn't know about it beforehand, it is karma. However, if you pick up that rock and think, "I must build something with it," then it is not karma. With your lama, one cannot tell whether it is karma or not. It might be, but he may have had a reason to pass into nirvana at that time, in which case it is not karma. Did he die because of your karma? No, it is not your karma. Now you don't have a lama because he has finished teaching you, so it will be up to you whether you practice or not. That's your karma. Because the lama has passed away, he is finished. All the previous Kagyu lamas passed away. All lamas die, all living beings die; there is nobody who won't die.

Question: An aspect of Buddhist practice that has been getting more attention in the West these days is social activism in which you bring your practice out into the community to make a positive change. There has been a growing interest in the socially active aspects of going from your meditation seat into the community and bringing about positive change. Some of the instructions of mind training could be interpreted as a sort of withdrawal from social activism, so that others are not given the benefit and opportunity of dharma.

Rinpoche: If everybody would practice these mind training instructions, it would really be good for everyone, including the community in general. For instance, it is beneficial for oneself, and if that person over there is doing it, then it is beneficial both for that person and everybody around. Mind training is very good for individuals and communities.

chapter two

THE PRACTICE OF THE PRELIMINARIES

I. THE PRELIMINARIES

I prostrate to the Great Compassionate One.

1. First, train in the preliminaries.

We begin lojong practice with a visualization and a prayer.

A. THE VISUALIZATION FOR THE MIND TRAINING LINEAGE

IN YIDAM PRACTICE OF THE VAJRAYANA we usually meditate, visualizing ourselves in the form of a deity or yidam. In mind training practice we just see ourselves in our ordinary form, but on the crown of our head we visualize our root guru who is the source of all our blessings. First, we visualize on the crown of our head a lotus flower which is untouched by any of the faults of samsara; on top of that we visualize a moon disc, and on top of that we visualize our root guru with a smiling face.

We visualize our root guru either in his or her actual form or in the form of Gampopa or Atisha, whomever we are most comfortable with and in whom we can generate the most faith. It is very important to visualize him or her with a friendly, smiling face and a resplendent body. The lama has great love and compassion for us, so the lama's face is seen with a beautiful and magnificent smile. To create great merit, we visualize the lama's body as being very brilliant and resplendent. We think of the lama as having great loving-kindness and compassion for all living beings and wishing that they all be free from suffering. This compassion and love is not limited to particular individuals, but includes all living beings. In this way, the lama's mind abides naturally in the sphere of reality (Skt. *dharmadhatu*).

Because it is also important to think of the lineage of lamas that came before our root guru, we think that the root guru embodies all the lamas of the lineage as well. There are three basic ways to visualize the root and lineage lamas: one is to visualize the root guru with all the lineage lamas stacked above him; another is known as "the great gathering," in which we visualize the root guru with all the lineage lamas surrounding him like a great crowd; a third way, called "the precious way in which all are subsumed into one," is to visualize the root guru as the essence of all the lineage lamas who are subsumed into him or her.

While visualizing the lamas, we keep in mind all the enlightened qualities of kindness and compassion possessed by our root guru. While doing so, we supplicate our lama. Sometimes we say prayers to the lineage lamas, asking for blessings from our lama. We pray that we can achieve the kind of loving-kindness for all living beings and the compassionate wish for all of them to be free from suffering which are held by our root guru. We pray that these qualities of the lama are born in us as well. Then with great faith and devotion to our lama, we say this prayer:

> *I prostrate to the Great Compassionate One*
> *Whose form is the compassion of the Buddha and his*
> *children.*

You are the incomparable lord of dharma with whom any
*   relationship is meaningful.*

My root guru, you embody the life-breath of this lineage.
I pray to you from the depths of my heart.
Bless me with the full development of love, compassion
*   bodhichitta,*
And the ability to dismiss and dispel (all obstacles).

With this prayer we then visualize the lama coming down through the top of our head and entering a tent in our heart where he resides. This causes faith and devotion to increase. It is very important at the beginning of any meditative session to generate great faith and devotion in the lama and to ask for blessings in this way.

Having received the blessings and generated great faith and devotion, we sit in our meditation posture with our back straight and simply pay attention to the passing in and out of the breath. We don't try to regulate the breath, but breathe naturally, staying aware of the breath going out and coming back in. We count the in-breath and out-breath as one. We do not count out loud but are just aware. On our rosary we pay attention to the passing of the breath in and out for twenty-one counts.

We should do this very carefully because this is said to be the vessel for Shamatha practice. We should just be very mindful of the breath going in and out and not consciously think, "Now it is going out; now it is coming in," or the other way around. Very carefully and mindfully we pay attention to counting to twenty-one and then starting at one again. It is very important to make a container for Shamatha practice.

Above is the visualization for the preliminaries. Now comes the actual explanation of the preliminaries, which begins with the contemplation of the four thoughts that turn the mind, also known as the four ordinary foundations.

B. The Four Ordinary Foundations

1. The Difficulty of Finding a Human Birth

The sutras are primarily concerned with the instructions on how to reflect upon impermanence. In addition to reflection on impermanence, the great siddhas of India added three additional reflections: the preciousness of the human body comprising the eight freedoms and ten riches, the consequences of karmic actions, and the negative quality of cyclic existence or samsara. First, we all have this incredibly valuable human body which is much better than an animal body. Of course, an animal can behave nicely and have a kind attitude, but can an animal receive teachings and reflect upon them? Can an animal practice deep meditation or samadhi? Can an animal liberate itself from the causes of samsara? There is no way for an animal to receive teachings as a human can. Not only do human beings have the ability to listen and to understand the teachings, but they also practice intelligently and understand what they are doing. When you think about it, this is of immense value. The preciousness of the human existence is not just a belief, it is really true. If we reflect upon this, then there is an actual reason to rejoice in the immense wealth of having a precious human body.

Milarepa [5] said that one does not really need to read about the four ordinary foundations in a book; one only needs to look around and see that impermanence is obvious everywhere. We have the precious human body now, but it does not last. Everything is impermanent. It is clear that we have reached a very special circumstance now in having this precious human life. We can see that this precious human birth is a great opportunity. But if we do not use it, then it is a complete waste. What a shame to squander this opportunity! We can see that a human birth is very precious and that it is important to use it as such. So the first contemplation is on the precious human existence and all its possibilities.

2. Death and Impermanence

The second contemplation is on death and impermanence. If we sit and think about death and impermanence, we are bound to become a little sad. Most people think it is not a good idea to sit around and think about something which will upset us. But actually, it is a good idea because if we do not think now about death and impermanence, one day they will definitely arrive anyway and then we will not be prepared. Not knowing what to do and what will come next, we will experience great suffering, whereas if we start thinking about impermanence now, while we still have time to find skillful means to deal with it, then later we will not be caught unaware. Even though in the short term the contemplation of death and impermanence might cause discomfort, in the long term it will actually save us from greater suffering.

3. The Infallible Law of Cause and Effect (Karma)

The third contemplation is on the infallibility of karma, which is cause and effect. The word "karma" is often understood as a fate that is impossible to change or alter. But that is not the Buddhist concept of karma. The Buddha taught that one can do something about one's karma. Happiness and suffering are created by karmic actions; they are the results of actions; and these actions are the result of our choice of what we do. We cannot change the results immediately, but we can still change the new causes that we create with our behavior.

All living beings want to avoid suffering, but we need to understand that negative karmic actions cause suffering, so if we try our best to avoid creating new negative actions, then their effect which is suffering will diminish. Living beings also want happiness, but we need to understand that wholesome or positive karmic actions bring on happiness. In this way, karma is not out of reach, because we can do something about how karma will ripen for us later on. As practitioners we should definitely take it upon ourselves to avoid what is unwholesome and to do what is meaningful and good.

So in this contemplation we contemplate that if we do virtuous actions, then the effect or result is happiness; if we create a cause of non-virtue by performing a negative act, then the result will be suffering. So there is a way of overcoming suffering in life, and this is by creating virtuous causes which can only arise by pursuing a path of dharma.

If we have doubts about these four contemplations, it is said that it is very helpful to recite prayers like the Seven-Branch Prayer[6] in which we take refuge, generate bodhichitta, confess, dedicate the merit, and so on. When doubts arise, this is a very important and beneficial practice.

4. THE INHERENT TRAGEDIES OF SAMSARA

The fourth contemplation is on the inherent tragedies of samsara. The inherent nature of samsara is that there is always something wrong and this is true for everyone. All living beings suffer in one way or another. But it doesn't have to be that way. We don't have to continue suffering. We can overcome not only the causes of suffering, but we can overcome the entire environment of suffering, which is samsara, by making use of the instructions of mind training on the relative level and the instructions of Mahamudra on the ultimate level. Reflecting upon the negative quality of samsaric existence inspires us to want to overcome suffering and to attain liberation and be free; it makes us want to put more energy into mind training and Mahamudra practice.

Milarepa said, "I do not study what is written with black ink." Rather, Milarepa studied everything as it actually is. We can also just look around and see how things are. All living beings are born, grow up, age, become sick, and pass away. We can also observe the consequences of actions and what is painful in all different ways. All this is observable if we pay attention. But we can also see what is truly valuable: a precious human body, which can lead us to embrace a spiritual path by understanding what it means to cultivate spiritual qualities and to practice. Such a person is very precious. When we acknowledge that we have this preciousness, we can rejoice in that.

Also, we will be inspired not to leave it at that, but to put it to use with a lot of energy, enthusiasm, and perseverance. That is a special way of studying the dharma through understanding how things are.

From time to time a student will say to me, "I like the dharma and am interested in practicing, but I feel that it is difficult for me to practice. I cannot really get into it. What should I do?" I suggest, "Spend some time reflecting upon the four thoughts that change the mind—the precious human body, impermanence, karma, and suffering." This is not like training in Shamatha and Vipashyana, but more a reflection, thinking about how things are: Are they permanent or impermanent? We spend time working with these four topics in our mind. These will cause inspiration, in which case we feel that it is not difficult to practice. This is why the first of the seven points of mind training is the preliminaries, or the foundation, for any and all practices that follow. If we have that foundation of having reflected on the four thoughts that turn the mind, we are then able to proceed with every practice that comes afterwards.

When we train in the teachings of the seven points of mind training, we still have some problems. Sometimes these problems can take the form of happiness, success, and good times and sometimes the form of difficulties, physical and mental pain, and misfortune. Success becomes an obstacle when we are affluent, have lots of satisfaction, and everything goes well. This causes a tendency to forget the dharma practice because everything is fine; we just go along and get caught up in it, forgetting our usual practice. That's a problem and, therefore it is called "the obstacle of happiness." The other obstacle comes when we experience misfortune, failure, or physical and mental pain. We could also forget dharma practice then because we are too caught up in being depressed, and so forth. As a matter of fact, we can use both situations for mind training and in that way become more even-minded so that we are neither depressed during difficulties nor carried-away by success. In this way mind training lifts us during difficulties and grounds us during success.

Questions

Question: You said we should visualize our root guru either in his or her own form, or as Gampopa or Atisha. I always visualize him either in his own form or in the form of Vajradhara. So should we visualize him in this case as Gampopa or Atisha?

Rinpoche: There are several ways of visualizing one's root guru. For instance, it is fine to visualize him as Vajradhara because Vajradhara, having all the qualities of the Buddha, is stainless. One can also visualize one's own root guru as he or she is if one has complete faith and confidence in him or her. But sometimes because we are very familiar with our lama, we can lack complete faith and devotion and, therefore, tend to see faults in our root guru. When this happens, we can visualize the root guru in the form of Gampopa or Atisha, because these teachings of mind training come from Atisha, who passed them down to Gampopa. These individuals lived far in the past, so never having met them we cannot possibly see a fault in them.

Question: As a student new to Buddhism I have not developed a strong connection to a root guru. How does one practice in that case?

Rinpoche: Well, the one for whom you feel faith, devotion, and respect no matter which individual, should be your object of refuge. That is whom you visualize.

Question: You taught that it is necessary to supplicate the guru with deep devotion, as well as to follow his instructions. When the root guru dies, do we continue this practice to create openness and further devotion, further commitment, or is there some actual living quality of the root guru? Is there a Buddhafield that the root guru is part of, a sort of energy field, or does the practice just help us follow the instructions more clearly, more devotedly?

Rinpoche: Whether your lama has passed away or is still living doesn't really make a lot of difference because the point is the strength of your faith, devotion, and prayers. For instance, Milarepa often prayed to Marpa and many of his spiritual songs start with prayers to Marpa, though at the time Marpa had already passed away. It is said that if one has enough faith, sacred relics (Tib. *ringsel*)[7] will issue even from a dog's tooth! This refers to the story of an old woman in Tibet whose son was a great trader and was always going to India. The mother was very old, and when her son was to go to India she said, "Oh son, you are always going off to India. It is such a wonderful place. The Buddha was there, as well as many great saints. It would mean a lot to me if you would bring me back some kind of relic from this holy land." The son went off to India, had a lot of work to do, and totally forgot the relic. When he returned, his mother asked, "What did you bring me?" The son said, "Oh. I'm so sorry. I forgot all about it." The next time he went she said again, "Please don't forget. Please bring me something from India." Again he got really busy and forgot it, leaving her very disappointed. Then came the third trip. Once more the son had so much to do that he forgot. The fourth time the mother said, "If you forget again, I will know that you don't really love me at all; in fact, if you don't bring me something this time, I am going to die in front of you." He went and again became very busy and forgot. But this time, just before reaching home, he remembered and thought, "Oh no! I completely forgot. What am I going to do? My poor old mother! She is going to die in front of me." He was really in despair and looked around frantically for something to give her. Seeing the dried up skull of a dog lying there, he approached it, thinking: "I just have to get her something. She is going to die in front of me if I don't. I can't let this happen." So he took a tooth out of the dog's skull, wrapped it very nicely, and went home saying, "Look mother! You are really lucky today. You are very fortunate. I have brought you a tooth of the Buddha himself." His mother was so pleased that she put it on the shrine, made many offerings, and prayed to it. One day ringsel came from that tooth. Now ringsel can be produced from the tooth of the Buddha, but not from a dog's tooth. So it was her great faith and devotion and the power of mind which made that happen.

EIGHT FREEDOMS AND TEN RICHES

THE EIGHT FREEDOMS (Tib. *dal wa gye*)

The first four freedoms involve the human realm.
1. Not holding wrong views
2. Not being born in a primitive border land
3. Not being born in an age without a Buddha present
4. Not having all the physical faculties complete, such as being deaf or mute

The next four freedoms involve the non-human realms where attaining enlightenment is not very possible.
5. Not being born in the hell realm
6. Not being born a hungry ghost
7. Not being born an animal
8. Not being born a long living god

THE TEN RICHES OR ENDOWMENTS (Tib. *jor wa chu)*)

These ten conditions make it conducive to practice.
1. Taking human birth
2. Being born in a Buddhist place
3. Having intact senses
4. Being free from extreme negative karma
5. Having faith in the dharma
6. A Buddha has appeared
7. The Buddha has given teachings
8. The Buddha's teachings continue to exist
9. There are people still following the Buddha teachings
10. Having compassionate feelings for others

chapter three

AROUSING BODHICHITTA

II. THE MAIN PRACTICE

THE MAIN PART OF THE MIND training practice is concerned with bodhichitta. Bodhichitta is a Sanskrit word which literally means "awakened mind." It refers to the desire to help all living beings achieve complete happiness. Living beings, by the way, refers to all beings who have a mind, so this includes animals as well as beings we cannot see, such as hungry ghosts, jealous gods, and beings in the god and hell realms. Generally, there are two kinds of bodhichitta: relative bodhichitta and ultimate bodhichitta. Usually, it is taught that ultimate bodhichitta is more important than relative bodhichitta. However, because we are beginners in the mind training teachings, it is taught that relative bodhichitta is most important, while ultimate bodhichitta is only briefly mentioned. The practice begins with a brief teaching on ultimate bodhichitta. We begin with visualizing the lama as explained previously, reciting prayers to him or her that we might receive blessings, and counting the breath twenty-one times so that we become proper receptacles for training in ultimate bodhichitta.

A. ULTIMATE BODHICHITTA

We begin with ultimate bodhichitta followed by relative bodhichitta. The reason Chekawa Yeshe Dorje decided on this order is because relative bodhichitta is the desire that forms the noble intention to proceed with developing ultimate bodhichitta. The dualistic mind is not very stable and to work with something that is so unstable is very difficult to do. Wouldn't it be better to stabilize the mind in real meditation or samadhi? To train in absolute bodhichitta first and later train in relative bodhichitta based on the stability achieved? Then relative bodhichitta will be more lucid, clear, and steady so that progress is more likely. That is the reason why absolute bodhichitta is discussed first.

Generally speaking, there are two types of meditative training: analytical meditation and resting meditation. We usually begin with analytical meditation, which is inquiring about the nature of phenomena, beginning with external phenomena as explained in *The Heart Sutra* with the statement, "No eye, no ear, no nose, no tongue" and so forth." When we examine the nature of phenomena, we fail to find any phenomenon which truly exists, so everything is regarded as dream-like. This then leads to the first instruction:

1. ANALYTICAL MEDITATION

2. Regard all phenomena as dreams.

The word "dharma," here translated as "phenomenon," is used in many different contexts. Sometimes it refers to teachings and sometimes to a particular practice or a specific quality that we try to cultivate in our practice. But in this particular context, the word "dharma" doesn't mean the teachings, rather it means any perceivable object or entity, such as an external sight, sound, smell, and so forth. These are not as they seem: they are visible or perceivable but not truly existing, just like dreams. Therefore, first understand that all phenomena are dream-like and then train in regarding them as being so.

I don't feel that it is necessary to spend a lot of time in this teaching discussing emptiness and whether things are real and concrete or do not exist as real and solid as they seem. As a matter of fact, they can be taken apart into smaller and smaller parts until they are atoms. However, even the smallest particles cannot be established to truly exist as something concrete and real. This can be arrived at through intelligent reasoning from the Middle Way philosophy. Using Middle Way logic, it is possible to show that all phenomena are not as real as they seem. This method proceeds by proving that every view we hold about reality can be disproved. Another approach is to establish how things are, rather than disproving their reality.

The nature of the emptiness of phenomena can be illustrated with the example of a dream. Every one of us dreams at night, and while we dream, it seems that there are objects, sounds, and so forth, which are exactly the same as they are while we are awake. We see hills, forests, houses, people, and so forth, during our dreams, but these phenomena are not as they seem. They appear to us, but they are not solid even though we can hit them, fall off them, and so on. Is everything we see in our dreams there? No. When we dream of a house or mountain, there is no real house or mountain in the room. In other words, while not existing, these phenomena still appear. How is it possible that something that doesn't really exist still appears to us? The answer is that it is like a dream, when we see, hear, feel textures, taste, smell, and so forth though these things are not really there. How should we regard the phenomena in our waking state? As empty just as in a dream. We therefore should "Regard all dharmas as dreams."

Sometimes we contemplate that all outer phenomena—trees, houses and mountains—are not real, but resemble appearances in a dream. We also contemplate that the inner phenomenon of our mind, which perceives all outer phenomena, is also not real. Rather, our mind is empty of inherent existence.[8] To engage in the two contemplations that outer and inner phenomena resemble a dream, we first think that everything we see in the animate and inanimate world is like the appearances arising in a dream and that our sensations of these phenomena—smell, taste, touch, sight, hearing, and feeling—are also like the sensations felt in a dream.

To repeat, we think that everything we perceive outside of us is not real; it is like a dream or an illusion. If everything out there is just a dream or illusion, then these phenomena must come from the mind. The next thought is, "Well, is the mind itself real?" To determine if mind is a real, solid entity or empty just like outer phenomena, we can, employ the Mahamudra or Dzogchen instructions[9] to look directly at our mind. This practice of looking at mind is explained in the next instruction:

3. Investigate the nature of unborn awareness.

Looking nakedly at the essential nature of mind,[10] we find that mind is not established as any "thing" at all. This means that if we look for the mind, we find it has no color or shape, or any other definable characteristic which an object does. Since objects have a beginning, we may wonder, "Where does the mind start? Is there a point of origin for the mind?" Again if we look, we cannot find a point of origin for the mind. Other than thinking that it is like the wind moving in the sky, there is nothing to indicate what it is like. Since there is no place where it begins, it is said that mind is unborn.

If mind is unborn, we may then ask, "So where is it now?" Examining the present mind to see whether it is somewhere outside the body, we find that there is no place where it resides in the objects that we sense or see. It is not separate from the body, so we ask, "Well, is it inside?" But we cannot find a particular place where it is located in the body. Since mind does not have a color or a location, we therefore say that it is by nature empty.

Finally we wonder, "Where does mind stop when thoughts stop? And where do thoughts go?" Again, there is no place we can find where thoughts end. The mind does not attach itself to an outer object and stop there. There is no origin of mind, it does not dwell anywhere, and it does not end anywhere because it is empty. So the mind is without birth, abiding, and cessation. This awareness can't be found. This contemplation of looking for the mind, trying to find if it has any reality or not, is a very important practice to do over and over again until we are convinced that the nature of mind is emptiness.

So, first we examine outer phenomena to establish that they are like a dream; then we look at mind itself and see that it is without birth, abiding, and cessation. From this we establish that the inner phenomena of mind are also empty. But this thought that mind and phenomena are empty is just another thought, so now we must look at the person who has that thought with the next instruction.

Let us examine what the perceiver is, what we call "me." Actually, when we look for it, we cannot find it anywhere; we fail to find it, and yet at the same time it seems that there is someone. This lack of finding is here called "unborn," which means it doesn't come about nor does it exist right now; it didn't arise and it doesn't abide anywhere in the present. This is exactly what we need to look into in order to find that this also does not really exist, which is called "empty of essence" or "empty of identity."

Earlier, two different types of meditation were mentioned: analytic meditation,[11] and resting meditation. Analytical meditation which uses rational thinking, is not the method meant in "investigate the nature of unborn awareness." Here, the instruction means to look at unborn awareness. This is like observing birds, just seeing what they are doing. Where do they live? How do they get there? How do they fly about? What do they eat? Inquiry is simply taking a look by observing. In exactly the same way, we take a look at the mind and ask: Where does it dwell? How does it behave? What does it look like? What color does it have? What shape does it have? And where is it? How does it move? How does it stay? And so forth. This type of inquiry is not intellectual.

From time to time we have the feeling that the mind is steady and remains calm. Then when we take a close look at it, what is it really that remains calm now? We fail to find that there is someone or something that remains. In the same way, sometimes we notice that there is thinking, and when we look into the identity of what is it that thinks, we fail to find that there is a thinker, someone or something actually thinking the thought. This is not some kind of rationalization, but something we see when we look. This is what is being taught here in the statement: "Investigate the nature of unborn awareness." Unborn here is a synonym for absence of identity.

4. Even the antidote is released in its ground.

We begin with the belief that everything is solid and real. Then we develop the belief that this is incorrect and everything is just emptiness or like a dream. This second belief, however, developed by the previous instruction, is not real either. To illustrate this point, Shantideva gave the following example: If you were dreaming that you had a son and the son died, you would think, "I had a son and now he is gone." You might think that the thought that he is gone is an antidote to the thought that he existed. But in fact this can't be correct because none of it is real: it is all like a dream. So the thought that you had a son was not real, and the thought that your son had died was also unreal. That is what "the antidote released in its ground" means. When you begin to believe that everything is emptiness, then you have to let that thought go, too. You have to look at the one who is thinking that thought and realize that this one, too, is not real.

In his commentary on *The Seven Points of Mind Training*, called *The Great Path of Awakening*, Jamgon Kongtrul said that this teaching is explained as conceptual meditation because examination of outer objects as having no birth, no abiding, and no cessation is done through using our intellect.

As previously mentioned, there are two ways of meditation training: the analytical meditation of a scholar, a pandita, and the resting meditation of a kusulu, a simple meditator. Analytical meditation of a pandita involves questioning, inquiring, and quoting the scriptures from masters of the past. To gain some certainty about how things are, we need to look at external things to see how they are, and we need to look within to see how our mind is. We even look at the remedies against the usual belief about outer and inner phenomena. As we reach some kind of conviction, all we can see is direct experience. Then comes the next training called "resting meditation of a simple meditator." The above instruction concerns analytical meditation, while the next instruction concerns resting meditation of direct perception.

2. PLACEMENT MEDITATION

5. Rest within the all-basis, the essential nature.

What does the all-basis, the alaya, mean? We have the eight consciousnesses:[12] the five sensory consciousnesses of sight, hearing, smelling, tasting, and body sensation; the sixth mental consciousness, the seventh afflicted consciousness, and the eighth alaya consciousness. We do not rest in the sensory consciousnesses because these are externally oriented. We don't rest in the sixth mental consciousness which is thinking mind, engaged in thoughts of the past, present, and future. These six consciousnesses are sometimes present and sometimes not. For example, our eye consciousness will not be present or functioning when our eyes are closed or it is completely dark. Does this mean that when the consciousnesses are not present, we die or turn into a stone? No, because there is an ongoing sense of the present and a lucid knowing quality of mind. This knowing, or awareness, is the eighth alaya or all-ground consciousness. The alaya consciousness has the quality of being always present and the quality of knowing. The quality of knowing or luminosity (Tib. *selwa*) is always there whether we are awake or asleep or dreaming; it is a conscious quality that is never interrupted.

I once had an operation in which they gave me an anesthetic. I experienced the sensory consciousnesses all being interrupted and there was no physical sensation and at the same time there was this lucid quality which was not interrupted. I think this was the eighth consciousness and this is what we need to rest in.

There are two aspects to the eighth alaya consciousness: the consciousness aspect called the *kunzhi namshe* in Tibetan, and the wisdom aspect called the *kunzhi yeshe*. What is the difference between these two aspects? Even though the wisdom quality of the eighth consciousness is ongoing and unimpeded, we may not be aware of the emptiness of phenomena. Not realizing this characteristic of phenomena is called the consciousness or *namshe* aspect of the alaya. This ignorance forms the foundation for the other consciousnesses. However, with meditative training we see that even though there is no entity there, (i.e., when we look for this consciousness, nothing is there), present at the same time is this conscious wakefulness, the wisdom aspect of the eighth consciousness. Our task as a practitioner is not only to rest in the nature of this alaya, but also to be aware of its nature.

When we use the word *alaya*, we usually mean this eighth consciousness. But in this particular instruction, to rest in the nature of alaya points to our basic Buddha nature (Skt. *tathagatagarbha*). This instruction means looking without any conceptualization at the nature of mind. This Buddha nature is complete simplicity; it is the union of emptiness and luminosity. It is luminosity because it has the characteristic of wisdom, and yet it is not an object or thing. The nature of this luminous clarity is emptiness. So this is the practical application of the meditation: just to look at the nature of mind, at that unity of clarity and emptiness.

In the meditation on ultimate bodhichitta, we look at the nature of mind and find there is nothing at all that we have to think about or fabricate. We do not have to think that something that exists does not exist; nor that something that does not exist, does exist. We just look at the nature of mind.

Once we have finished the looking, we can recite the Seven-Branch Prayer as we did in the preliminaries. After practicing meditation on relative bodhichitta (the analytical meditation) followed by meditation on ultimate bodhichitta (resting meditation), we must dedicate the merit of this practice.

3. POST-MEDITATION

6. In post-meditation, regard all beings as illusions.

The first four instructions already given in this chapter explain how we should engage in the analytical meditation training of a pandita as well as doing resting meditation of a simple meditator, a kusulu. Once we understand this, we persevere in this training and meditate more and more. But, a conflict can arise. A practitioner might think, "If I meditate, then I can't work and do my job. And if I do my job,

I can't practice." This is why there is this fifth instruction distinguishing between the meditation period and the post-meditation period. During the meditation session, we train in analytical meditation or we simply do resting meditation. During the post-meditation stage we are involved in activities, such as going to work, having conversations, and walking about. How do we deal with these activities? When things go well and there are no problems, we become very excited and happy, and when things do not go well and there are problems, we worry a lot and wonder, "Oh no! What is going to happen? This is terrible," and so forth. Rather than reacting to these events we should train in the understanding we have from mind training, namely, that whatever we perceive is like a magical illusion. So the reaction of being excited about success or depressed about failure will diminish when our external world is seen as a magical illusion.

This completes the teaching on absolute bodhichitta. In summary: The first instruction was about external phenomena, "Regard all phenomena as dreams." The second instruction is about inner phenomena, the perceiving mind, "Investigate the nature of unborn awareness." The third instruction is, "Even the antidote is released in its ground." Then we come to the resting meditation of the kusulu, "Rest within the all-basis, the essential nature." Finally, the instruction is on how to practice during daily activities, "In post-meditation, regard all beings as illusions." In this way, absolute bodhichitta is practiced using these five instructions.

B. RELATIVE BODHICHITTA

In the teachings on relative bodhichitta, there are three parts: the preliminary part, the main practice, and the post-meditation practice.

In *The Seven Points of Mind Training* we are in the section on the main practice, which has two parts: absolute and relative bodhichitta. In these teachings the relative aspect is emphasized more strongly, because relative bodhichitta is of immediate importance for the practitioner. It is what occurs in daily life. We train in meditation to realize the emptiness of external phenomena and the emptiness of internal phenomena. However, in mind training, we act as if there is a personal identity and as if other persons are also real. So relative bodhichitta is making believe that there is a self and others.

We begin with a special instruction from the Master of Sumatra, Jowo Serlingpa. He said that when you plant the seed of a flower in a very nice and clean ground, the seed will grow very poorly. If, however, you plant it in moist and dirty ground enriched with manure, the seed will grow well. In the same way, just as a seed grows in dirty soil, to realize emptiness and develop an altruistic motivation, the bodhisattva will grow and progress in confused and messy situations.

When it comes to promoting the bodhisattva's frame of mind, we need to consider two attitudes most people hold: one is called "goodwill" and the other, "ill-will." It seems most people alternate between these two. "Goodwill" means that out of a good heart one wants to help and further what is valuable, beneficial, and helpful. But sometimes we have ill-will and want to hurt and harm others. When it comes to engendering the bodhisattva attitude, goodwill is more helpful than ill-will, so as a practitioner we are advised to cultivate the attitude of goodwill as much as possible and to diminish and reduce our ill-will. Why? Because when we become used to an attitude, sooner or later it manifests; sooner or later it expresses itself not only in words but in actions as well. When we consider what beings actually need, it is not ill-will at all; they need goodwill. For someone aspiring to be a bodhisattva, it is suggested that they cultivate and maintain goodwill and try to diminish ill-will.

Another reason is that goodwill helps both others and oneself. If one expresses goodwill, it immediately helps others and indirectly, sooner or later, there is feedback that helps oneself. So it also helps oneself to have a benevolent frame of mind to help others. Ill-will, on the other hand, immediately hurts others and indirectly hurts oneself as well.

Now, where do ill-will and goodwill spring from? They spring from either regarding ourselves as being most important or from regarding others as most important. If we look at the feeling, "I am important!" It can become the basis for many problems. If one regards oneself as being more important than others, sooner or later one will express this in ways that are harmful to others. But regarding others as important will sooner or later be beneficial for others and for oneself, too. Therefore we should try our best to develop the attitude of thinking of others as more important than oneself.

This is where mind training enters because one's basic attitude can be remedied with mind training. Why? Because predominant habits of considering oneself as more important than others can be changed: we can train in developing the attitude of wanting to help others and in diminishing the idea that we are more important than others. This is very beneficial. We can train in that further and further so that finally there is not much self-importance left in our own mind but we have the remaining attitude of wanting to benefit others. This is the real basis for mind training.

The main practice of mind training is forming the bodhisattva attitude which eliminates the tendency to treasure oneself as more important. Absolute bodhichitta obliterates the basis of self-cherishing because it is seen that the ego and personal identity are manifesting and bodhichitta is the solution. Therefore, it is said that training in absolute bodhichitta completely eliminates self-cherishing. But for a beginner it may not be so easy to be successful doing this. Therefore, it is more practical to put more emphasis on relative bodhichitta: we take the bodhisattva vow and commence in training to be a bodhisattva, especially by studying such wonderful and beautiful texts like Shantideva's *Guide to the Bodhisattva's Way of Life*. This text explains the benefits of developing bodhichitta, how to do so, the different kinds of training involved, and the negative consequences of ignoring the importance of becoming a bodhisattva.

The Seven Points of Mind Training may not be as detailed as *Guide to the Bodhisattva's Way of Life*, but for a beginner it is more applicable because the *Guide to the Bodhisattva's Way of Life* does not clearly mention how to begin practice, whereas the *Seven Points* does. In that way, *The Seven Points of Mind Training* is more practical and useful for a beginner.

1. THE PRELIMINARY PRACTICE

The preliminary practice of relative bodhichitta is to meditate on love and compassion for all living beings. Since this is difficult to do, we begin by generating love and compassion towards our mother. The way to start is to visualize our mother in front of us.

In modern times, when we look at the world, we like to think that in general everything is improving—that people's conditions are improving, that wealth is increasing, and that things are getting better. But sometimes it is very obvious that something is wrong. One of the ways we know this is true is that in these times some people do not like their mothers. Even though we love our mother, we sometimes become angry with her. If we think about it though, our mother has been incredibly kind by giving us our life and then sacrificing a great deal for us.

When we think about our mother, we should think about how much our mother did for us. We think, "When I was first born, I did not know how to walk. I did not know how to speak. I did not know how to put food into my own mouth, or how to go to the bathroom. I did not know anything. And my mother was the one who took care of me. In fact, I would not have turned into a person at all had she not taken care of and helped me. She put food into my mouth, she took me to the bathroom, and she put on my clothes. When I got a little bigger she would say, 'No, don't do that, it is dangerous.' She taught me everything that is necessary to become a proper human being."

Of course, sometimes our mother became angry at us and she may have even spanked us. But again, we couldn't understand at that time why that happened. It wasn't because she didn't love us or she had some kind of malice towards us. It was necessary because she was teaching us. If she hit us, she did not hit us because it was of some benefit to her; if she scolded us, she didn't do so because she liked it. It was all for our benefit and was the result of a great kindness to us.

In this practice we first feel compassion for our mother with the thought, "May she be freed from all suffering," and we show love for her with the thought, "May she have complete happiness." This text on mind training gives us the oral instruction to start with our mother and gradually extend compassion to all the rest of the beings in the world. We extend this compassion (May all living beings be freed from all suffering) and this universal love (May they possess all happiness) to the point where we regard all beings impartially.

That was the preliminary. Now we come to the actual meditation, which is the sending and taking meditation (Tib. *tonglen*).

2. The Main Practice of Relative Bodhichitta

7. Alternately practice sending and taking; these two should ride the breath.

The first instruction of practicing relative bodhichitta is that sending and taking should be practiced alternately. This is an instruction we actually follow. The practice shows why we should give-up self-cherishing and regard others as more important. It does not use reasoning or deduction; rather, it is very simple advice on how to begin. We begin by imagining other living beings in front of us, many or just a few. We can imagine people in pain, people we know who are sick, people in distress or suffering. We imagine that we send these people happiness and the causes of happiness as well. For this to happen, we imagine that we give them whatever goodness we can think of, and we imagine that we receive whatever suffering and causes of suffering, all the distress and negative emotions they experience. We imagine that by being freed from suffering and its causes, they experience happiness and well-being. We practice this again and again and thus become more and more used to taking away the suffering of others and giving them our own well-being and causes of happiness. By training in this sending and taking practice, the regarding of oneself as more important than others diminishes and regarding others as more important becomes stronger and stronger.

Moreover, the traditional instructions help us to become accustomed to a more positive way of thinking. It is not just our imagination, but we join it with our breath. When we exhale we imagine (or visualize) that our merit, our well-being, our physical and mental happiness, whatever fortune we may possess is sent out to other living beings in the form of our white exhaled breath and it touches the others who become filled with whatever goodness we have sent them. We imagine they are freed of any burden they carry and are happy and well. As we inhale, we imagine that anything troubling them (their negative emotions, their suffering, their problems, and so forth) leaves them in the form of dark light and we inhale it, taking it upon ourselves. Immediately, they are freed from the burden and we imagine them at ease, happy and calm. We practice that again and again.

We train in this meditation, called *tonglen* in Tibetan, to diminish our self-cherishing attitude and become more caring for others. In doing this practice we may worry, "If I give away all my merit, happiness, and well-being to others, I will not have anything for myself. Not only that, I may get sick and suffer from taking on the suffering of others." When things don't go so well for us, we may then think, "Well, this is because I practiced giving and taking too much. I was too concerned about taking on the suffering of others and now these terrible things are happening to me." But there is no reason to worry because we do not really exchange the karma we haven't created, with karma created by others. Karma cannot be transferred or eliminated by giving and taking practice, so we don't need to worry at all.

We may have another fear: "Well, what is the use of practicing giving and taking if it doesn't help alleviate the suffering of others or bring them happiness?" The answer to this is that we do not do this practice to bring about an immediate result in the other person. The purpose of this practice is to diminish our clinging to self-cherishing and to increase the attitude of benevolence and loving-kindness. Sending and taking training does accomplish that. Because the more we think of giving away our own happiness, well-being, and merit, the more we diminish the concern for "only me." The more we train in giving happiness to other living beings and taking on their suffering, the more the virtuous qualities of loving-kindness, compassion and bodhichitta will grow within us. When these qualities have become stronger and stronger, we will then be able to directly help others substantially. So sending and taking helps ourselves, because the more we are involved in benevolent activities for others, the fewer problems we create for ourselves. Also it helps us as well as others. Maybe it doesn't help immediately, but ultimately it becomes the cause for helping others. It is possible that sending and taking can help others immediately, however, it is not guaranteed.

3. THE POST-MEDITATION PRACTICE

8. Three objects, three poisons, and three roots of virtue.

The training in giving and taking should be practiced alternately with the breath and should be done during the meditation session. Therefore it belongs to the meditation practice of relative bodhichitta. But there are also instructions to use sending and taking during post-meditation. The instructions say, "Three objects, three poisons, and three seeds of virtue." When we move about in life, we see, hear, taste, smell, or touch an object that is pleasant, we become attracted to it and, as a result, form an attachment to this object in our mind. When, we notice that this has happened, our next thought should be: "May this represent the attachment of all living beings, and may all living beings be free of this attachment that is formed and overcome in my mind. May all beings experience happiness that arises from being free from this attachment."

We form this attitude and formulate the noble wish that all living beings be free. On the other side of the coin, we may see something unpleasant or hear something annoying and become irritated or angry because of an unpleasant encounter. If we notice that anger or aggression is forming in our mind much like an attachment, we should then make the wish: "May this represent the anger and aversion of all living beings, and may all living beings be free of anger and aversion, and may all beings experience happiness that arises from being totally free from anger and aversion."

We may also be neither attracted nor repelled by something; our mind remains blank and we are absent-minded. If we notice this indifference, we should then make the wish that the blindness or stupidity of all living beings melts into our mind and that they are then free from their ignorance. We formulate our wish: "May this be the end of ignorance of all living beings and may they all have the happiness that arises from being free of ignorance."

In this practice, "the three objects" refers to those objects that provoke our emotions of attachment, aversion, or indifference, while "the three poisons" are the emotions of attachment, aversion or aggression, and stupidity. Then we imagine that all living beings negative emotions dissolve into the emotions we have as they arise; and peace and virtue are formed with the wish, "May all living beings be free of negative emotions." In this way, the three poisons are transformed into the three roots of virtue. This is the practice of relative bodhichitta that we do during post-meditation.

9. In all your activities, train with these words.

In addition to relative bodhichitta in our post-meditation experience, the text says, "In all activities, train in these instructions." We put our words into action so that when we meet others who are better off than we, who are happy, who do good actions and so forth, rather than being jealous or competitive, we make the wish: "May they have happiness and may they progress in what they do. May their activities increase."

When we meet others who don't do anything special, we make our wish: "May they progress, may they give rise to the noble attitude of bodhichitta. May they have happiness."

When we see others who are suffering, we make the wish: "May they be free from suffering. May they be quickly relieved of the causes of suffering and experience peace."

When we meet people who are actively involved in creating causes for suffering by hurting others, we again make the wish, "May they quickly stop doing so and attain happiness."

We do not only pray when we meet such people but also when we hear about them; even when we just think about them, we make our wishing prayer.

These instructions do not mean that we only make good wishes because there are situations in which we can actually help others to increase their well-being, to remove their distress and suffering. If we are able to do so, then there is a chance to do something to help other beings, so why hold back? We can do it on the spot. It may be impossible to help them but that doesn't mean we can't give rise to the attitude, "I might not be able to alleviate the suffering of this person in this moment, but when the chance comes later on, may I be able to do so." We can hope and formulate our wish like that, praying to free others from suffering and to provide them with happiness.

10. Begin the sequence of sending and taking with yourself.

There is one more instruction for daily activities in the section on the post-meditation of relative bodhichitta. It has to do with not being able to help someone in great need and distress. We may not be able to help them, but we can still help someone who is not that terribly distressed and troubled. We can begin by feeling for a friend in trouble and need; we can begin with someone close to us. Having begun, we begin to focus and gradually become capable of helping others afflicted with suffering until finally we are actually capable of benefiting all living beings.

This practice of sending and taking should be done both as actual sending and taking meditation on the breath, and also as part of our normal daily activities. For instance, any time that we have a feeling of strong attachment, we should think, "May all beings be free of this feeling of attachment." If we are suffering or sick, or something terrible happens causing mental or physical pain, we should think, "May all living beings be free of such pain." If we become angry at someone, we should think, "All living beings feel this. May they be free of such hatred and anger." In the same way if we do something very good, then we should think, "May all living beings enjoy this virtue." If something very nice happens to us and we are very happy, we should again think, "May all living beings experience this happiness."

No matter what we are doing, we can practice this mind training. It is very beneficial to actually say the words, "May all living beings have happiness; may all living beings be freed of suffering."

Questions

Question: In the United States there are a number of mothers who whip their children for reasons that are not beneficial. When I use the instructions to teach the practice of compassion in abused families, it is very difficult for me to talk about that section because people who have been greatly injured say to me, "That doesn't make sense and it is not true."

Rinpoche: First of all, the meditation doesn't necessarily have to be on the mother. The point is to meditate on somebody who has given as much loving-kindness and help. Whoever that is, it is okay to start with them. Nonetheless, it is usually a mistake to think that one's mother is not kind. Think back to the first year of life when you were completely helpless. If it weren't for your mother, you would certainly have died. When the child grows and develops some kind of consciousness of self, then it can begin to have trouble with the mother. The mother might say, "You must eat now," and you answer, "No, I don't want to." Then trouble starts. The child does not want to do what the mother says and gets angry, and the situation starts from there. It seems to me that still there is something wrong with the idea that the mother is not kind because there is something very natural that comes from a mother with her baby: "This is my child." There is a natural protection and tendency to want to protect that child.

Psychologists have a very good motivation and really want to help. People are very unhappy and have much mental suffering, so psychologists and psychotherapists try to fix that suffering, to make it better. This is all very wonderful. But sometimes there can be a problem when they try to find out what causes the suffering or what the source of the pain is. The patient answers, "Well, my mother did this to me." The therapist answers, "That's it! That's the source of your pain. It comes from your mother. She's the one." I think that this is not necessarily true.

Question: I have a question about taking and sending. When you are taking in the negativities of others, what do you do with them? Do you dissolve them into emptiness or into the ground?

Rinpoche: In this teaching it is said that you just imagine that all the non-virtue and suffering dissolve into you, and nothing more is said about it. But there is another way to do it, a special way in which you visualize yourself as Chenrezig with a white letter HRI in your heart. That HRI is very hot and has the nature of flames. When you visualize taking on all the suffering and non-virtue of all beings, you visualize it as a black cloud that comes to you and goes in through your nose and down into your heart center, where the HRI burns it up. So all the suffering and non-virtue of all beings is burned up. When you are sending forth all your virtue and well-being, you visualize that it goes out in a white mist that spreads to all living beings, and they become very pure and endowed with great happiness.

Question: Let's say a thief comes into the shrine-room and hears the statement, "Regard all phenomena as dreams," then goes down to Brunswick and starts stealing money from all the stores. When the policeman arrests him, he says, "There is no theft, there is no thief, nothing was stolen. These are all dreams." But there is a problem if the policeman is not a dharma practitioner. So what should the policeman do or say?

Rinpoche: Here is what the policeman should say: "Yes, everything is illusory and unreal, like a dream, but there is still human feeling, even though it is dream-like. Therefore, there is also the dream-like experience of being imprisoned."

Question: If we are frequently faced with a wrathful person who really wants to destroy us, what is the most effective method of coping with this problem? Is it better to do Tara practice, taking and sending practice, or some kind of wrathful protector practice ?

Rinpoche: Whether you do Tara or protector practice, the result should be the same. The most beneficial practice is the taking and sending practice and the practice of patience. Sometimes it is not possible to have this much patience, and if that is the case, then the best thing to do is to stay away from the person. If there is such a strong case of animosity, when that person sees you, the animosity will just increase and nothing good can come of it. At that point the best thing is just to stay away from that person or situation and the sooner it is forgotten, the better the situation will be.

chapter four

TRANSFORMING UNFAVORABLE CIRCUMSTANCES

III. HOW TO CARRY THE PRACTICE ONTO THE PATH

A. THE GENERAL PRACTICE

11. When the world is filled with negativity, transform adverse conditions into the path of awakening.

WE HAVE DESCRIBED THE MEDITATION of wishing all of our good fortune, happiness, and virtue to be given to other living beings, and taking all the evil, suffering, and causes of suffering of all living beings onto ourselves. This is the main meditation, but in our daily lives many things often happen unexpectedly, such as a surprise illness. Then the question becomes, "What do we do about these things? How do we meditate in situations where we are happy and situations when we are suffering?" This is the meaning of "transform adverse conditions into the path of awakening."

Sometimes it seems that the world is filled with negativity and that living beings have much suffering and many accidents befalling them. We must learn to transform these negative circumstances into the path to enlightenment. This can be done in two ways: through the practice of relying on relative bodhichitta and through the practice of relying on ultimate bodhichitta. The instruction describing relative bodhichitta is described in the following section.

1. Relying on Relative bodhichitta

There are two aspects to relative bodhichitta when we are practicing using troubles and difficulties as a way to bring us along the path to enlightenment. The first has to do with diminishing self-cherishing and the second has to do with increasing one's sense of valuing others. The first aspect of diminishing self-cherishing can occur in situations when we go through difficulties and hard times. The instruction is:

12. Drive all blame into one.

When something bad befalls us—maybe we become sick or injured or have great mental suffering, because people gossip about or insult us—we always tend to put the blame on others by thinking, "I didn't do anything, yet this person has really hurt me," or "This has happened to me. Why has it happened? It is not my fault." We always put the blame on other people or outside circumstances. But in mind training we should do exactly the opposite. We should not think that the blame lies outside ourselves, but that the fault is ours. We should think the fault comes from holding ourselves to be precious, from believing, "I am important." We believe that the self is important when it really isn't.

Self-cherishing has to do with the sense of self, "This is me." But what this "me" or "I" refers to is not so certain. People may use "I" to refer to the body, other times to the mind. It is not that clear. In terms of the knowledge that realizes egolessness, there is a certain way to question the validity of the belief that there exists such an entity called "I." But that is not in the scope of relative mind training;

we just take it as a given that if there is this belief, then it is the problem and not the object of that belief. Selfishness is anchored in the belief "I exist." It is the main cause of our unhappiness. Thinking, "I am important. I am special," is the basis for so many problems, for so much selfishness and negative emotions. Sometimes anger arises, sometimes hatred or sometimes attachment and desire, sometimes pride and conceit; sometimes it is jealousy, sometimes stinginess, or sometimes close-mindedness. These emotions are allowed to take a foot-hold because they are nourished by the belief in "me," by regarding "me" as so special. As a matter of fact, sometimes the sense of "I" is regarded as the single and most important entity in the entire world: "I am incredibly important and valuable!" That is what is called "self-cherishing," which is regarded as what is to be eliminated in the practice of mind training. We may think that self-cherishing is some intrinsic component of our being, but it isn't. It is just a thought that pops up, and that is why it can be eliminated.

The difficulties that we have at present are all brought on by self-cherishing. Whatever problems we have, the amount of suffering they cause is directly related to how strongly we regard ourselves as being important. Even the more general and large-scale suffering of samsara—birth, old age, sickness, and death—is ultimately caused by self-cherishing, by ego-clinging. This is why whenever we go through difficulties, we can rightfully blame self-cherishing as the main cause of the problem.

I want to give an example about how it is that taking the self to be real is the true enemy. The story in question is about the great teacher Patrul Rinpoche, who lived in Kham. One time he was traveling with a servant to Central Tibet. They had a lot of money with them. The reason they were carrying so much money was that they were going to Central Tibet to offer butter lamps, make statues, and do many other virtuous things. The two were traveling alone across the Chang Thang Desert which was notorious for its thieves. At night they couldn't sleep because they feared someone was going to steal the money, so they suffered terribly. And in the daytime they were constantly looking around, ahead and behind, wondering, "Are the thieves going to come? Where will they come from?" It was extremely difficult.

One day Patrul Rinpoche thought, "I'm really not having a good time. It is so hard. What is the actual cause of my having such a bad time on this trip?" Then he realized, "It's the money. If I didn't have all this money, I could rest at night and travel comfortably. I wouldn't have constantly to look over my shoulder to see if a thief is coming." While he was thinking this, his servant was walking ahead looking out for the thieves and robbers while Patrul Rinpoche was behind. "Well, it's really simple," he thought. "This money is the source of the trouble and I am going to get rid of it." With that, he threw the money into the river, thinking, "It's gone now. That's great. Now I'm really happy." So he went along while his servant was still watching out for the thieves and robbers. Finally he said to his servant, "We don't have to worry anymore. The thieves and robbers are in the water." The servant said, "What do you mean 'the thieves and robbers are in the water'? They are everywhere." Patrul Rinpoche said, "No, I threw the money in the water. That was the real source of our problem." This illustrates that the problem was an internal attachment to the money, rather than the outside robbers.

The problem is we are so attached to a solid self which is, in fact, really empty. Shantideva said, "Whatever harm, fear and suffering there are in the world come from taking the self to be real. This is such a great demon. What will it do to me, this clinging to a self?" This demon has to be tamed. The demon of believing the ego to be real has to be subdued.

13. Be grateful to everyone and everything.

"Be grateful to everyone" means to try to understand that others give us kindness. First of all, this is easiest to practice when people are nice and we have a pleasant and enjoyable time with them. Then we think, "I had a good time with so-and-so." It is very easy to think others are very nice when they are kind to us. But when others are nasty, hurt our feelings, or disappoint us, we complain, "This is so frustrating, so disheartening, disappointing. I am so tired, both mentally and physically, of spending time with so-and-so." This shows quite clearly that we are not capable of doing mind training at that time and instead just blame the other person. On the other hand, there is a way to deal with this, namely by using the opportunity when people are unpleasant to cultivate patience, tolerance, and compassion. We actually see that they provide us with the opportunities to practice and cultivate positive qualities, and we should be very thankful to them for this.

In other words, when people hurt or harm us or throw obstacles our way, we should regard these as an opportunity for practice. It is an opportunity to practice because it offers the chance to use our patience, our willingness to carry through and develop our compassion. These frustrating people are actually kind by providing us the chance to progress on the path. Acknowledging and appreciating this kindness is a way of making use of the difficulties on the path to enlightenment, which comes under the heading of contemplating the great kindness of everyone in order to increase cherishing others.

This is a way to reduce self-cherishing and a way to increase cherishing others in order to bring difficulties into the path of enlightenment. These two aspects fall under the training of relative bodhichitta.

There is another relevant quote from Shantideva's *Guide to the Bodhisattva's Way of Life* :

> *If the road is covered with rocks and thorns,*
> *you can either pave the entire road with leather,*
> *or you can take a piece of leather*
> *and place it on the soles of your own feet.*

This example shows that the world is filled with suffering which you cannot stop by trying to pacify all the different negative forces and obstacles. What you can do is protect yourself. This protection rids you of clinging to a self. That is the same as covering the soles of your feet with leather, rather than paving the whole world with it.

In another quote Shantideva says, "All the suffering and bad things that happen in the world come from this clinging to a self." The Buddha taught that one should not consider oneself to be more precious than others. Rather, we should consider others more important and more precious. From beginningless time, throughout samsara, we have considered ourselves to be more important and more precious than others, and this has brought about all our obstacles and suffering. Therefore, this attitude is what we must eliminate. The whole problem is based upon holding others to be more important than ourselves.

So the citations from Shantideva concerned reliance on relative bodhichitta. The next lines deal with relying on ultimate bodhichitta.

2. RELYING ON ULTIMATE BODHICHITTA

To rely on ultimate bodhichitta is to realize emptiness, and to understand that all suffering and negativity actually lack reality. It is like being carried away by water or burnt by fire in a dream; the suffering in that dream is not real. It is the realization of the emptiness of phenomena, the realization that life is a dream that leads to realization of ultimate bodhichitta. The instruction for this is:

> *14. Seeing delusive appearances as the four kayas is the*
> *unexcelled protection emptiness gives.*

The way to see confusion as the four kayas[13] (four bodies or four dimensions) is to regard any difficulties and troubles we may experience as a dream, a magical illusion, because the true nature of external phenomena has no inherent nature:[14] external phenomena of samsara are like phenomena in a dream: they do not exist and the realization of this absence of true existence is the dharmakaya. While phenomena do not exist ultimately, on a relative level, due to mere dependent origination, they arise like appearances in a dream and this is the nirmanakaya. These two qualities of being non-existent and yet perceived or experienced are an indivisible unity which is the sambhogakaya. The unity of all three kayas or dimensions is the svabhavikakaya. In this way, we can train in treating confusion as the four kayas, which is how they actually are. This method is called "the unexcelled protection of shunyata or emptiness."

If we have developed some stability in our meditation we may be capable of dealing with problems and mishaps by regarding everything as an illusion, the nature of the four kayas. Otherwise, we will have to train in the relative level of dealing with difficulties by bringing them into the path of enlightenment, diminishing self-cherishing and increasing cherishing others.

In addition to this instruction, there is the following practice called "the special application of bringing difficulties into the path of enlightenment."

15. The best method entails four practices.

Calling the four practices the best method means that these four are methods for eliminating all pain and suffering for oneself, and bringing happiness and benefit to all beings. this is possible through the following four methods.

a. ACCUMULATING MERIT

The first practice is accumulating merit. We can ask, "Is it really possible to rid ourselves of suffering and create circumstances which are conducive to the practice of dharma?" The answer is that this is possible because all things have a cause, and the cause of happiness is virtuous activity. To create this cause of virtue we must first accumulate merit.

Where does the fortune of good health, prosperity, and enjoyment come from? They result from the ripening of wholesome karmic actions in the past, primarily that of a noble intention, but also noble physical and verbal behavior, showing respect to noble objects, being generous to those in need, and so forth. All these are the accumulation of merit. When we train in creating merit, we insure that positive circumstances will follow and negative circumstances will subside.

b. CONFESSION OF NEGATIVE DEEDS

To accumulate merit, we also need to be freed of our previous negative karma. To do this we must engage in confessing our negative deeds, which is done through the four powers.[15]

Situations have repercussions called "the ripening of karma." One of the ways to reduce the ripening of karma is through regret for having created the causes that bring on suffering. This is one of the main special applications: to confess or acknowledge negative actions. The Tibetan word is *shagpa* and has the sense of chipping away, e.g., when chopping down a tree one starts bit by bit until nothing keeps it from standing any more. In the same way, regretting and acknowledging are the opposite of justifying our self and our rigid actions. As long as we hold on to our entrenched attitude, it is impossible to change. On the other hand, if we loosen up our attitude, feeling regret for what we have done, then we are able to let go of that pattern, slowly changing our ways. This is why confessing for having done something negative is the second of the special applications.

For example, if we have the attitude that killing is good, or that it is our job and we earn a lot, every time we have that thought, it solidifies and becomes more and more difficult to change. On the other hand, if we start thinking, "Maybe it is not so good to kill again and again. This will not help me in the long-run. It will make things very difficult and also hurts others." That kind of attitude will weaken the severity of karma. It will also make the ripening of the negative karma of killing less strong.

c. MAKING AN OFFERING TO GODS AND DEMONS

When we encounter obstacles, whether from other persons or non-humans, we should practice the three methods.[16] If someone dislikes us and harms us, we usually retaliate. But when we think about whether anger will solve the problem, we will realize that it will not. If someone is angry at us and does something hateful, and we get angry and want to retaliate by saying mean words and fighting, the only result is that this person will become increasingly angry and cause more harm. Whether the obstacle is caused by a human or a non-human force, it is clear that by reacting with anger or revenge the situation will only get worse. Therefore, the correct thing to do if someone harms us is to be patient and compassionate. In these circumstances the other person's reaction can only decrease in strength, whereas if we react in the same manner as they, the conflict will only escalate. Our sole option, then, is to meditate on patience and compassion.

When we request a Vajrayana initiation, a torma is usually offered at the beginning to all demons and obstructing forces, because it is possible that they may try to create some kind of obstacle to our receiving the initiation and doing the practice. This torma is a symbol for what we have just discussed: the fact that if harm or an obstruction occurs, it cannot be pacified by anger, retaliation, or resentment towards the person causing the harm. As a token of this truth, a torma is offered before the initiation to all the non-humans present as a symbol of peace and friendship, an offering of bodhichitta so that no obstacles arise. Whether we are dealing with a human or non-human, or someone who really dislikes us, the only way to address the situation is to defuse it by sending forth love and compassion.

d. MAKING OFFERINGS TO DAKINIS AND PROTECTORS

Dakinis and dharma protectors are friends to us and will not create obstacles. Offering torma to the protectors is like offering help to a friend and receiving help in return. In the same way, if you make offerings to the protectors, they will help you. So whether we are dealing with dakinis and protectors, people or friends, if you help them, they will reciprocate.

A beginner may have difficulties understanding what dharma protectors are. Usually we talk about our protectors as the Three Jewels, the Buddha, the dharma, and the sangha. But in the Vajrayana, in addition to the Three Jewels, there are the three roots: the gurus, the yidams, and the dharma protectors. The lama is called "the root of blessings." We might ask, "How could there be anyone more exceptional than the Buddha? The Buddha is the most eminent source of refuge and object of supplication for blessings." But it has been over 2,000 years since Buddha Shakyamuni lived on earth, so we may feel a gap between the Buddha and us that we cannot bridge. It is still possible, however, to receive blessings because there is a lama or guru who carries the Buddha's blessings and we can connect with them in the present. When we receive the teachings, we receive the blessings of the Buddha: it is the same as having received them from the Buddha personally. This is the reason why the lama is called "the root of blessings."

The second type of root are the meditational deities or yidams in Tibetan. It is said that there are 84,000 ways to practice the dharma to achieve the goal of enlightenment. We can't possibly practice all of these and so in the Vajrayana path, the dharma practice is condensed into the form of a yidam. By practicing the yidam meditation thoroughly, we can achieve enlightenment and so the yidam is called "the root of accomplishment."

The third root is called "the dharma protectors, the root of activities." Usually the sangha performs the duty of dispelling hindrances and of providing good circumstances for people to progress on the path. But the sangha is not only incarnated as human beings. The noble sangha constitutes the Buddhas and bodhisattvas on a high level of realization, endowed with the blessings, the abilities, the great qualities, wisdom, and so forth. It is not confined to human beings. Dharma protectors are also able to manifest in many other forms and also in the Buddhafields. When they are requested to act, they will engage in activities that are beneficial for the dharma. There is a tradition for calling upon the protectors of the dharma to carry out these activities. They are summoned, visualized in male and female forms corresponding to whether they represent wisdom (female) or skillful means (male). They may take on other aspects, too. When we talk about the three main qualities of enlightenment as wisdom, compassion, and power, then it is capability that manifests in the wrathful form, compassion in the peaceful form, and so forth. Sometimes protectors are painted in *thangkas* and sometimes they are part of our visualization. But when making a request or supplicating them to act on behalf of the dharma and beings, we accompany this request with a torma offering. This is said to be beneficial for dispelling obstacles and for providing conducive circumstances for dharma practice. That is why the fourth point from among the special applications is giving torma offerings to the protectors of the dharma.

There is a practice called *Chö* (often spelled "chod"), the practice of severance or cutting through, which is sometimes done in this context. It is done to eliminate the clinging to a self which we consider precious. When we cling to this self, we are mostly attached to our body. To cut that attachment, the Chö practice includes the visualization of offering one's own body to others. In this visualization, we invite all the gods and demons to come before us. We imagine a multitude of them—some in peaceful form, some in wrathful form—appearing in front of us, and we offer up our own body to them. Sometimes we visualize that we actually cut our body into pieces and offer it to them to enjoy. Other times, we can visualize that we flay our own skin off and then offer our body to them.

There are two methods of offering our body in Chö practice: one is called "the white offering" and the other "the red offering." In the white offering, we imagine that we cut up our body, which is transformed into wonderful and delicious food with the five flavors and aromas. We then offer this transformed substance to the guests. In the red offering we imagine our body in its present state. We visualize that we cut it up and offer it as it is to the gods and demons.

The reason for employing these four methods when we encounter negative circumstances, such as illness or hostile attacks, is to eliminate the belief that we are more important than others. To summarize, the four methods are accumulating merit, making confessions, offering tormas to gods and demons, and offering tormas to the dakinis and dharma protectors.

16. Whatever you meet, instantly join it with meditation.

The previous practices were mainly those engaged in during the meditation session. The next instruction discusses the post-meditation state when we bring unexpected circumstances to the path. Whatever we encounter should be brought into the path, in other words, made use of. For instance, when we have a pleasant moment that we enjoy, we make the aspiration, "May every being experience happiness." This is the way we help promote loving-kindness and compassion. Then there may be an unpleasant moment or situation in our life and at that time we remind ourselves that the unpleasantness of this difficulty has to do with self-cherishing. We make the aspiration, "May self-cherishing diminish in me and in all living beings." In this way both pleasure and pain are brought into the path.

Questions

Question: "Rinpoche, how should one apologize and be sorry for misdeeds? Also, how long should one keep feeling sorry for misdeeds? *Rinpoche*: As mentioned earlier there is what is called "the four remedies of powers," one of which is called "the power of remorse." This is to actually acknowledge that what is not good is not good, and not just pay lip-service. When we really understand that something that was nasty was nasty – and not in an artificial, fabricated way—then that is the limit to which one should carry the practice.

Question: Rinpoche, I would like some examples under what is referred to as "contemplate the great kindness of everyone." For example, a project needs to be completed and people are not keeping to their responsibility, so they are not following through on what they are supposed to be doing. *Rinpoche*: In the Buddhist sense of training in compassion and patience, the main component is that we need to be intelligent about how we are compassionate and how much we are willing to tolerate. So, we shouldn't let people get away with something that is stupid just because it is difficult for us to confront them. That is not what is meant here. For example, if your house is burning down, you shouldn't just sit down and say, "Oh, this is difficult. I should be patient." We are allowed to say something. If it is true, then you tell the truth.

Question: When we talk about self-cherishing, how do we exhibit patience and forbearance? What would be the behavior? How would we demonstrate it?

Rinpoche: The example I gave of the house burning is quite a good example, I think, because it is pretty useless to be patient in the sense of not doing anything. You can bear it while doing something about it intelligently, in other words, you use water to put out the flames.

But in the case of people acting in a way that is inappropriate, you don't have to tolerate their not doing what they are supposed to—that is not what is meant by patience here. Because if you say something like, "Hey, you aren't doing something you are supposed to," they might change and do a good job. Patience has to do with your not being angry with them for not doing what they are supposed to. Anger doesn't necessarily help them, but telling them may help.

Question: Rinpoche, my question goes back to what you spoke about earlier, about sending and receiving practice. Would you describe further how to begin and end that practice in general?

Rinpoche: It is perfectly all right just to send and take in an instant, without much preparation and ceremony. It is also all right to use the traditional method of first beginning with aspiration prayers, guru-yoga, visualizing Chenrezig and so forth. It is also alright to do it in the traditional way. But if one doesn't use a lot of elaborate details, it is also fine.

Question: It seems there are situations in which it is better to say something to others and to stop being angry than to absorb the anger. Is this teaching sometimes more a mental practice than a practice actually carried out?

Rinpoche: It is okay if you can say something. What I was referring to is your mental attitude, that you should not say something angry back. If you get angry in return, things will become worse.

Question: It is said that anger is the worst of the disturbing emotions. I never really understood why anger is worse than passion or stupidity.
Rinpoche: The other disturbing emotions, such as passion, pride, and jealousy do cause harm, but it is more gradual. For instance, if you have attachment and only think about pleasure and good things, it will eventually become a cause of suffering. The same thing with pride, thinking, "I am so great!" Right then and there nothing terrible is happening, but eventually it will become the cause of suffering. However, anger and hatred are immediate. The worst part is the actual harm done to self and others. Anger and hatred that do not cause outright actions such as hitting and harming others, but cause the thought, "I would like to destroy him or her," constitutes what we call a "black mind." This black mind is more immediately negative than other disturbing emotions and is therefore said to be the worst.

Question: I've heard that some illnesses can be caused by external forces. In that case, is it true that these forces can be pacified? What is torma and how can a lay person like me actually offer a torma?
Rinpoche: Some illnesses can be caused by demonic forces; it is also said that nagas can cause sickness. A good way to pacify them is by offering torma, but the Chö practice visualization is best. Visualize the demon and imagine that you are offering your body. It may appear to be superstitious, but it really helps.

Question: What if a friend has a serious illness? What can be done actually to help a person with cancer or some other life-threatening disease?
Rinpoche: Sometimes one can help, but there are cases where nothing can help, just as doctors cannot cure everything. Sometimes mantras, medicine, and visualizations can help; sometimes they don't at all.

I guess you can never tell. My father passed away when I was twenty-five years old, and shortly afterwards my mother became very ill. She looked really very bad and her tongue swelled up terribly; it truly seemed that she was going to die. It was terrible for me to think that my mother would die so shortly after my father. We tried many things, many doctors, much medicine, and nothing worked. Then somebody suggested that a particular practitioner who was really good with mantras should come and help. So we called this man, but I didn't think anything would happen because he didn't look like he had any realization or meditation experience. All he did was say a few mantras and blow on my mother. But the next day she started getting better.

chapter five

MIND TRAINING IN DAILY LIFE

IV. PRACTICING MIND TRAINING IN DAILY LIFE

THE FOURTH POINT DEALS WITH the presentation of practice in our life, and is divided into two parts. The first part is how we practice mind training during our lifetime, and the second is how we practice mind training at the time of death.

A. PRACTICING MIND TRAINING IN OUR LIFETIME

17. Practice the five powers, the condensed heart instructions.

Practicing the five powers has to do with the teachings that the Buddha gave after appearing in this world. In order to alleviate the suffering in the three lower realms and the entire wheel of samsara, the Buddha gave many teachings and instructions which cover things that we can use in the way we behave and in our meditation practice. They are quite extensive and include the Vinaya precepts, which define conduct, and the Prajnaparamita, which are the teachings on transcendent knowledge. These teachings are part of the sutra teachings. The Buddha also gave the tantric teachings, of which there are many detailed sections, including kriya tantra, charya tantra, yoga tantra, anuttarayoga tantra, and many others as well.

The words of the Buddha were recorded in India and transmitted through the centuries, until they were translated into Tibetan, for the most part by eighth century Tibetan translators. So we can say that for the most part they still exist today, with a few small exceptions. The main part of all the teachings the Buddha gave are collected in the Kangyur, or the precious collection of the Buddha's words, consisting of around 103 huge volumes of teachings.

All these scriptures on the teachings of the Buddha are laid out according to the sutra or the tantric perspective. How does one know this? From the explanations given in the treatises by the great learned and accomplished masters of India and Tibet. The Indian masters, mahasiddhas, and other great teachers of the past condensed the teachings into treatises, explaining the meaning clearly and showing how to go about practicing them. This was done in Tibet as well by practitioners who applied the teachings, reached a level of perfection themselves, and then wrote from their personal experiences of what proved itself to be valid. All these teachings are called "the treatises," and were collected in the Tengyur. They still exist today. But when it comes to personal practice, there is what is called *men-nag* in Tibetan, which means "heart or pith instructions." They are also called oral instructions and they are used for personal practice. *Men-nag* means something that is precise, applicable, effective and can be used immediately, therefore, the pith instructions are what people usually practice.

These heart instructions flowed into Tibet from many sources. Let us take the tradition of the Kagyu Lineage. The Tibetan translator Marpa journeyed to India and connected with many great masters of those times: Naropa, Maitripa, and many others, from whom he received the heart instructions. They prophesied that Marpa would propagate the lineage. He not only received the instructions but practiced them personally to such an extent that he also attained realization and accomplishment. He brought the instructions back to Tibet and passed them on to his disciple Milarepa, who then passed them on to Gampopa and others. These three masters, Marpa, Milarepa, and Gampopa, are considered the foremost fathers of the Kagyu Lineage.

The achievements of Gampopa were predicted in the *King of Samadhi Sutra* where the Buddha stated that in the future there will be someone who will propagate the instructions and make "the king of meditation" flourish, be understood, and realized. Centuries later, Gampopa united the instructions from the Kadampa Lineage on mind training with those from Milarepa, who received the teachings of Maitripa and Naropa through Marpa. So Milarepa not only had the mind training instructions of the Kadampa, but also the instructions from Naropa, as well as the Mahamudra teachings, all of which Gampopa had combined in one.

These instructions have been transmitted throughout the centuries until today. A great master known as Jamgon Kongtrul Lodro Thaye insured that these oral teachings would not disappear from our world by writing them all down in a collection. It contains the instructions transmitted through the Kagyu Lineage and also the eight primary lineages called "The Eight Chariots of the Practice Lineage." He compiled them all into a collection of teachings known as *The Treasury of Pith Instructions*. In this collection of teachings, the seven points of mind training were placed at the front because he considered them very important.

Before Jamgon Kongtrul Lodro Thaye compiled his collection of works, another earlier master took up mind training and spread it widely. His name was Gyaltse Thogme; he also wrote his own commentary to clarify the seven points. In his commentaries, we can find very precise and helpful instructions on how to begin mind training, how to carry on in the middle, and how to complete it in the end.[17]

These heart instructions are of many types. Of course, it would be wonderful if you could practice all of them in a very vast and extensive way, but that is not always possible. Therefore, the word "condensed" is added here: it means putting together the most important points so that we are able to use them. This is the teaching here, "the *condensed* heart instructions." What are they? They are phrased here as "the five powers."

The instruction for the first practice of how to engage in mind training in this life is to train in the five powers, which are a summary of the essential instructions. We will now discuss these five powers as they relate to daily life, and then we will discuss these same five powers in terms of the time of our death.

1. POWER OF GOODWILL

To strengthen this power of goodwill to bring about more benefit we make a pledge, "I will practice for a certain amount of time." For example, when we do the preliminary practices, we say, "I want to complete these practices 100,000 times each, so I will begin with the 100,000 prostrations." That strengthens the power of benevolence or goodwill because we have made up our mind to do so. When going into retreat, we make up our mind and formulate our resolution, "For this amount of time, I will remain in retreat and practice one-pointedly." That is also very beneficial as a way of strengthening the power of bringing forth the benefit of goodwill. Even if we are not able to spend three years in retreat, we can say, "For this amount of time, I will practice." Or it could be applied in a different way "As long as I am alive in this body, I will refrain from doing negative actions" also has great strength. We may not be able to keep this pledge during our entire life, but at least we could say, "For this number of years, I will avoid these negative actions," or "For this number of months I will avoid them." That kind of mental resolve helps strengthen the power of goodwill.

Assume that we are bothered by a specific negative emotion, for example, the tendency to be angry, competitive, or jealous. Wanting to improve, we can aim our practice toward progressing in this particular area. When we wake up in the morning, the emotions have the tendency to reoccur and we notice this. So that is an opportunity to make up our mind in the morning: "Today I will work on diminishing this particular negative emotion (anger, for instance) which is problematic for me. I will try my best today."

Then we go about the day and before going to sleep at night we check, "How well did I do today? Was I successful or not?" Since we are an ordinary person, we may have been unsuccessful. Then we say, "Well, I didn't do so well. I will try a little more tomorrow." Again we make the commitment the next day. In this way, we use the power of goodwill to form the wish to do better. When we practice the seven points of mind training, the focus of the practice is to keep away from self-cherishing and trying to increase valuing others more highly in our lives. That could be the pledge we make in the morning and the examination we make in the evening, resolving again to do better the next day.

If we do not choose a specific negative emotion we take the general vow: "From today until I reach enlightenment, I will not be parted from either relative or ultimate bodhichitta."

We can also make this vow for a shorter time, even for a day. This gives power to our practice. For instance, if we are a very lazy person, we might wake up in the morning, thinking, "Today I really want to get this work done." Or if we have strong defilements and disturbing emotions, we would think, "Today I will not fall under the power of this." It is this kind of determination that is being talked about here. If we make a promise to ourselves, our practice is empowered.

2. POWER OF FAMILIARIZATION

The second power is that of growing familiar. We may think it is enough to have the first power of forming a good intention, but something more is necessary. We need to grow familiar with the practice and this comes about through training, not only during the meditation session but also during daily activities in post-meditation. We remind ourselves of the practice and stay alert to our behavior. Through this kind of mindfulness, we can improve and come to a sense of familiarization and progress. It is not guaranteed that we become immediately successful, because we may make mistakes. But that doesn't mean that we should be disheartened. The strength of the power of familiarization is that we are willing to continue the practice and grow. What we set out to do here is to try to overcome the negative emotions that arise in our state of being by applying the remedies against them. We also have to increase the qualities of loving-kindness and compassion. What causes us to progress in this endeavor is the power of growing familiar.

Here we think: "Whatever I do today, whether I am lying down, standing up, eating, walking around, or talking with friends, I will be extremely mindful not to let my bodhichitta diminish."

We start with this determination in the morning and based upon it, we remain as much as possible mindful of it all day long. Throughout the day, whatever situation comes up, we remember not to be parted from bodhichitta. In this way we become accustomed to this wish to help all others.

3. POWER OF VIRTUOUS ACTIONS

The third power is called "the power of virtuous seeds." It is like planting seeds to get a crop. This goes along with our training to diminish ego-clinging and self-cherishing and promote loving-kindness and compassion. Sometimes more fuel is necessary to help us move along. This fuel is the virtuous seeds. We do what is good, meaningful and wholesome in our physical actions. In our words and our attitude, we try our best to do what is good and noble: being generous to those in need, paying respect to the noble objects, reciting the sutras and making prayers, chanting aspirations, mantras, and so forth. Mentally we form the intention and let it settle in a state of equanimity, which is samadhi. In this way, we create virtuous actions which, in addition to the former powers, help especially when we dedicate the virtue to diminishing self-cherishing and promoting loving-kindness and compassion. We make that intention in the beginning and dedicate the outcome to that specific purpose in the end.

With this power, we should always strive to increase our virtuous activities of body, speech, and mind so that our bodhichitta is enriched. We pray: "If bodhichitta has not arisen in my being, may it arise. If it is decreasing, may it increase. If it is increasing, may it grow yet further for ourselves and others."

Whatever suffering arises in ourselves or others, whatever inauspicious circumstances, obstacles, or accidents come about, the only way to overcome them is by engaging in virtuous activity with our body, speech, or mind. This can include doing circumambulations,[18] offering the Seven-Branch Prayer, and other positive actions. These are the ways to overcome negativity. With strong determination and familiarization as the basis, we can go further and recognize that the seed of virtue in body, speech, and mind is this wholesome activity. This is the only way to overcome all the unfortunate things that can happen to us.

4. POWER OF REMORSE

The fourth power is the power of remorse. In these particular teachings remorse means identifying the trouble-maker, what causes conflict, suffering, and problems. We look at what really prevents us from being liberated not only from the three lower realms but from all of samsara. People have a tendency to be selfish. What is it that prevents us from being liberated and attaining complete enlightenment? It is this tendency to treasure "me" too much and too dearly. This is the largest obstacle on the path and gives rise to all the negative emotions that take us in. In other words, allowing this tendency to reign makes us unhappy again and again. When we are unhappy, we feel uncomfortable physically as well. Anybody spending so much time being unhappy mentally and physically doesn't have a happy life. The tendency to cherish the self so highly is our greatest fault. Once we are clear that ego and self-cherishing are to blame, it is much easier to deal with situations than simply accepting that we have a strong ego. An individual with a strong sense of self finds it difficult to be free because he or she strengthens that tendency on a daily basis. But here the training, rather than strengthen ego more, is to make it diminish until it vanishes. This is the outcome of the power of remorse.

When practicing mind training, sometimes obstacles arise and we feel that our bodhichitta is not increasing or that we aren't feeling compassion for others. This is an obstacle that does not come from outside of us; rather, it stems from believing we are so important. Sometimes we think, "Oh, I can't stand it if something bad happens to me. I can't stand this suffering. I only want to be happy." Or we are depressed, and think, "I can't do anything for others. This is too difficult. I can't help myself, much less others." The desire not to have anything negative happen to ourselves and the feeling that we can't possibly help others are the main obstacles to this practice. We have to recognize that these obstacles come from the belief that self is very important. When this happens, we should think: "From beginningless time I have wandered in samsara and experienced all sorts of suffering and difficulties. They have come from believing myself to be precious, from taking a self to exist where, in fact, there is none.

"All the suffering and all the non-virtuous actions I have committed come from this illusion of a self. Not only have I wandered in samsara since beginningless time, I am still doing so and, therefore, experience this difficulty. Taking myself to be so precious is the cause.

"Further, I have been cherishing myself for so long that I continue to amass negative karma. This will go on indefinitely if I don't stop.

"It is the thought of holding myself to be more dear than others that has resulted in this suffering. This habit of clinging to a self will continue if I let it and then there will never be any chance for true happiness.

"No matter what, I will destroy self-cherishing, which is the cause of all suffering."

This fourth power is often translated as "reproach," or "repudiation" of the fault. Actually, the word in Tibetan is a compound in which the first syllable means "wearing away." So any time that you have a problem or an obstacle, you recognize the cause, which is the clinging to a self. But you won't be able to get rid of your self-clinging immediately; you have to wear it away. As you accustom yourself to that process and gradually efface the notion that you are precious, bodhichitta will increase.

5. THE POWER OF ASPIRATION

The first four of the five powers serve specific purposes. When we begin, we are not yet able to engender virtuous qualities in our lives or in our spiritual practice, so at this point the power of good is important. When we cannot reduce the tendency of selfishness, it is important to bring forth the power of remorse. To develop remorse, there is a daily practice, which is the power of familiarization. Then there is the assistant, which is the power of virtuous seeds. The fifth power is a natural background that brings about the strength of all four, and this is the power of aspiration.

The power of aspiration is the pure mental wish we can make. As ordinary people, our mind does not have the strength to make this wish of aspiration come true immediately, but that's all right. The sincerity we put into the wish will insure that sooner or later the effect will materialize. Therefore, the power of aspiration is that we repeatedly make the wish: "May I become capable of eliminating self-cherishing. May I become capable of perfecting treasuring others as more important than myself." As we approach the force behind this aspiration, it actually manifests more and more like that, until it becomes an actuality in our mind.

This power of aspiration means that whatever virtuous activity we do, whatever meditation we do, whatever training in the instructions we do, we pray: "May my bodhichitta increase and come to include all living beings. May it also be born in all living beings. May it increase in those in whom it has been born, and may this increasing bodhichitta really come to benefit all living beings."

We make this aspiration prayer for the benefit of all living beings at the end of any virtuous activity we perform or after any meditation we do.

These five powers are a means to improve our practice of bodhichitta and increase our ability to get rid of all the obstacles that arise in our dharma practice. We should exercise these five powers throughout our lifetime.

We can transform our behavior into that of virtue by employing these powers, which are similar to the four previously mentioned. The first being the power in recognizing that the negative things we have done are indeed negative. Often when we perform a negative action, we are quite attached to it. For instance, if we have someone who is giving us a hard time, we may think, "Okay, today I'm going to go out and beat up that guy. I am going to be a hero and he is going to be ground into nothing." We become quite attached to this notion and we like it. So the first power is recognizing negative actions to be negative, which already decreases the force of that karma.

The second power is to confess non-virtuous deeds to someone else. If we are completely by ourselves, we can sit and think, "Oh, that was really bad. I confess it," That thought, however, has no great power. On the other hand, if we go to someone else and say, "I did this really terrible thing," then the confession has more power. So going to a lama or spiritual friend and confessing our negative actions has more power. If we can't do that, simply confessing in front of a shrine, a Buddha statue or stupa adds power to the confession.

The third power is relying on the remedy. This is the thought, "I did something really bad. To purify it I am going to do this which is really good." The third power means relying on a virtuous action to help clear away past negative action.

The fourth power is the power of resolving not to repeat the negative action. Sometimes we think, "I did this really bad thing in the past and I am truly sorry I did it, but in the future I might have to do it again." That, too, is not very powerful, so the fourth power is that of resolving, "I will never do that again." These four powers are the best method for purifying previous negative karma.

B. Practicing Mind Training at the Time of Death

18. The Mahayana instructions for transferring consciousness at death are the five powers; the way you behave matters.

1. Power of the Virtuous Seeds

These same five powers we have been discussing, (though in a different order), will also help us achieve bodhichitta at the time of death. The first of the five powers is the power of virtuous seeds. When we know we are going to die, the first thing we do is to give up all our possessions. We should rid ourselves of any attachment or clinging we have to our worldly things and give them with a happy mind to whomever they can most help, thinking: "May these be used by this person." We should do this without any attachment, thinking: "Because I was attached to many different things, the disturbing emotions of passion, attachment, ignorance, and so on, have arisen. Now I need to be rid of all these things, and so I give them without any attachment at all for whatever purpose they can best be used."

2. POWER OF ASPIRATION

Second is the power of aspiration. The particular aspiration here is: "In this life and in all following lives, may I not succumb to the tendency of treasuring myself as more important than others. May self-cherishing diminish. May I promote again and again loving-kindness and compassion." We can make this aspiration right now, but it is especially important to make when the signs of death begin to appear. We know that there isn't much time left so our sincerity increases and deepens. It is especially important to make that aspiration at this time.

Here we think: "Whatever virtue I have of body, speech and mind, may I, who have practiced mind training in this lifetime, not be separated from it in the intermediate state or in the next lifetime. May I continue to practice bodhichitta and may I not forget the teachings. In the next life may I meet with the teacher who taught me these precious things."

We pray to the lama and the Three Jewels to grant their blessings so that all of this may come about.

3. POWER OF REMORSE

Third is the power of remorse. The time of death is not an easy one, because we experience a great deal of physical discomfort and pain as well as mental anguish and unhappiness. Rather than feeling despair, we should identify the main cause of our suffering as ego-clinging and make up our mind that at this point: "I will try my best not to create the causes of the negative emotions and karma created out of self-cherishing. I will really try my best to diminish ego clinging from now on into all following lives." Understanding that we should not commit what causes suffering again in the future is the strength of remorse.

At the time of death we think: "Now I am at the time of death and am experiencing suffering. The cause is attachment to myself as being precious. In reality, there is no ultimate self; the mind is not solid and real and, therefore, there is nothing that actually dies. The suffering I am now experiencing comes from clinging to the idea of myself as precious. It is this that I must destroy."

4. POWER OF GOODWILL

The fourth power, goodwill, is the most important at the time of death. Whether we are in the *bardo*[19] or whether we are already in the next life, what is always of greatest benefit is loving-kindness and compassion—treasuring others more than ourselves. This attitude always brings benefit. Understanding this, we should make up our mind very firmly and sincerely: "At all times and in all places I will place special energy in bringing forth the qualities of loving-kindness, compassion, and the vow of a bodhisattva." If we have already trained ourselves in thinking like this now, then it will come back at the time of death, in the bardo state, and in future lives as well. But especially at the time of death, whatever comes to mind is much more acute and we really mean it at that time. Sincerity is much deeper at the time of death, so at that time we should especially take the vow of always placing special emphasis on loving-kindness and compassion.

At this time we pray: "May my bodhichitta increase at the time of experiencing the pain of passing away. May it also increase during the intermediate state between lifetimes, and may I experience it during the next lifetime. May I never be separated from this precious twofold bodhichitta."

The twofold bodhichitta comprises relative and ultimate bodhichitta. It is crucial to have a strong determination to engender bodhichitta at this time.

5. POWER OF FAMILIARIZATION

The fifth power of growing familiar must be practiced while we are alive. We make ourselves more and more habituated to reducing self-cherishing and increasing loving-kindness and compassion. Some practitioners die while in sitting meditation. If we cannot do that, we can die in the reclining position. The Buddha died in the position called "the reclining lion," where we place the right shoulder on the ground, one hand to the cheek, lying comfortably on our side. As we die, we gently let our attention remain in loving-kindness and compassion, making the strong wish to be of benefit to all living beings (relative bodhichitta), or to understand that all phenomena are just mind, like dreams, like magical illusions, like a mirage (ultimate bodhichitta). Passing away like this has tremendous benefit, not only at that particular time but also for future lives. This is the outcome of the fifth power of familiarization.

The second half of this instruction is, "the way you behave matters." It is very important how we actually pass away. Jamgon Kongtrul wrote in his commentary, "There are many instructions for practitioners on how to die, but this particular one, which utilizes the fivefold power at the time of death, is most wonderful." He praised it as being of special importance for practitioners to acquaint themselves with this way of passing.

At the time of death, we use the power of familiarization or habituation by thinking: "I have practiced bodhichitta and will not forget it, no matter what suffering I am currently experiencing. I will continue to practice bodhichitta during the suffering I am experiencing now, during the intermediate state, and in the next lifetime, I will not forget it."

It is very important that we make a great effort to practice bodhichitta now because when we are in the midst of sickness and suffering it is not easy to follow through. We have to rely on the force of familiarity to maintain our resolve during trying circumstances.

To be more specific: there are some methods we can physically invoke to help the practice. It is said that the very best thing we can do is sit in the sevenfold posture of Vairochana.[20] If that is not possible, we should lie down on our right side with our right hand on our right cheek, blocking the right nostril. This is because the winds of karma go through the right subtle channel and right nostril. The wisdom air moves through the left subtle channel, which is why the left nostril is kept open. With the air moving through that nostril, we meditate on sending and taking as much as we are able. These are the oral instructions of the Kadampa masters.

Questions

Question: If one has accidentally harmed someone and receives the fruition of that action because the person harmed takes extreme revenge, does it help the person to purify negative karma even if the original harm was unintentional? It seems to me that one is bearing the suffering that the other person can't bear by taking it. If that is really true, I am assuming one is purifying that karma.
Rinpoche: Actually, the only thing to do is to be patient, and then the result is beneficial for both. For oneself, the benefit is obvious: one doesn't create any more negative karma, and therefore one's patience represents purification. For the other person it is also beneficial because if you get angry at him or her, they will only become angrier still. By your patience and kindness, their anger may not decrease, but it will not increase, so it is helping them. And if their anger should decrease, your patience will have proven beneficial to them as well as to yourself. As to the second part of your question: even if the karma for your initial action is lifetimes long, I think that by bearing revenge patiently it could be cleared in this lifetime.

Question: I have a question about the five powers at the time of death. The bardo teachings say we should remain unattached at the time of death, but the five powers seem to suggest that we aspire never to be separated from our teachers or from bodhichitta. This seems to be a form of attachment and desire.

Rinpoche: These instructions are specific for the mind training. If you have very good meditation, then you can rest in the nature of mind at the time of death. That is another instruction. There is a strong reason for the mind training instructions: you can die in two states of mind, one very virtuous and the other filled with fear and anger. Everything that follows is based upon these states of mind. So if, as taught here, you die with an attitude of wanting to help others, of wanting to increase loving-kindness and so on, then the appearances of the bardo that arise at the time of death are peaceful, easy, and friendly. Based upon the continuity of a peaceful, loving mind, the next birth will also be good. But if you die in a state of anger or great fear, then the appearances that arise in the bardo are frightening and very troubled. That state of mind will continue influencing what comes next, just as it does in dreams. For example, when we go to sleep happy and at peace, then our dreams are happy, but if we have a troubled mind, say we fought before we went to sleep, our dreams are troubled. It is the same at the time of death. So it is very important to put our mind in a good place at that time.

Question: You said that if I die in a peaceful state of mind, the next birth will also be peaceful, but the intermediate (or bardo) teachings say that becoming liberated is best.

Rinpoche: If you really have a very strong foundation of meditation, then, of course, it is best to be liberated at the time of death. But without the ability to do this deepest kind of meditation, the best thing to do is to raise yourself by stages to the point where you will have the ability to train yourself to get there.

chapter six

THE EVALUATION OF MIND TRAINING

THIS SECTION ON THE EVALUATION of mind training shows the ways in which we can tell if mind training is working.

V. THE EVALUATION OF MIND TRAINING

A. CLINGING TO SELF AS A MEASURE

Evaluation means seeing whether or not our practice of mind training is going well. When we are involved in practicing mind training, there may be some results of the practice. If that is the case, it is good to acknowledge it; we can rejoice in that way. But since we are ordinary practitioners, it is possible that at times our mind training will not go that well. At that time it is necessary to acknowledge this so we can be more diligent in ridding ourselves of the negative forces and put more energy into promoting the good forces.

19. All the Buddha's dharma converges on a single point.

The first instruction is that all dharma, all the teachings of the Hinayana and Mahayana, have one common purpose: to reduce or eliminate the clinging to a self. Whatever dharma we practice, whatever mind training we meditate on, the purpose is to diminish that clinging. If our clinging doesn't diminish, then our practice isn't working properly. If we notice that the continual thought of ourselves as important is decreasing, it is one sign that mind training is working.

If we want to know whether our dharma practice is working or not, we have to examine it by asking, "Do I still consider myself to be important? Am I still clinging to myself as something precious?" For instance, if we had a piece of gold and wanted to know how much we had, we could not know this just by looking at it. We would have to put it on a scale and weigh it. Similarly, measuring our clinging to self is a way of telling if our dharma practice is working. Is our clinging to the self diminishing or increasing?

It is said there are 84,000 kinds of dharma, which are too numerous to understand and practice fully. For instance, if practitioners in the main vehicles of the Hinayana, the Mahayana, and the Vajrayana do not have a thorough understanding, they may have the impression that the Hinayana or Shravakayana is very different from Mahayana and even more different from the Vajrayana. This is not a correct view because all of the Buddha's teachings agree.

Let's look at the first turning of the wheel of dharma that emphasizes the Four Noble Truths. The first noble truth is the most important one with the other three being additional truths. The first noble truth is the truth of suffering; the others are the truth of the origin, the truth of the path, and the truth of cessation. It is said that we should understand the truth of suffering, which has four aspects. These are impermanence, suffering, interdependent origination, and egolessness of person. In other words, the main intent of the first turning is the understanding that the personal identity of a self is non-existent, and that the main practice is to develop realization of egolessness. In this way, the main intent of the first turning is cultivating the knowledge that realizes egolessness, which is the direct remedy against ego-clinging.

In the second turning, there are many sutras, namely, the Prajnaparamita sutras which focus on egolessness. We know the condensed form of the Prajnaparamita sutras, the *Heart Sutra,* states, "There is no eye, no ear, no tongue," and so forth, to show that all phenomena are empty and devoid of having a self-entity. The purpose of the egolessness of phenomena and the main aim of a bodhisattva in this second turning is to develop relative and absolute bodhichitta, as well as training in the six perfections, to realize emptiness. Why? Because understanding emptiness is the direct remedy for clinging to a self, there is a direct relationship between the first turning of the Shravakas and the second turning in the vehicle of Mahayana.

In the Vajrayana, the main practices are called the creation stage and the completion stage of the yidam deity. In the creation stage, rather than having the ordinary concept of oneself as being just "me," with an ordinary body that is impure and a mind that is influenced by disturbing emotions and ego-clinging, we train in the mandala of the yidam deity, which is completely pure. We identify ourselves as pure, totally free of ego-clinging and negative emotions, a non-samsaric state. That is the direct remedy against ordinary clinging to self. Our environment is not samsaric but a pure Buddhafield; our dwelling place is not an ordinary house but the mandala of the deity; our body is not an ordinary body but the pure enlightened form of the deity; our voice is the enlightened speech, and our state of mind is the deity's awakened mind. This is a training that is the direct remedy for the ordinary way of clinging to oneself as being an impure, ordinary, samsaric being. In the completion stage, we dissolve everything into emptiness and remain with our mind resting in the nature of mind, the nature of all phenomena. This is the direct remedy for ego-clinging, believing there is a solid personal identity.

In this way, there is complete agreement between the first, second, and third turnings of the wheel of dharma. The text says that all levels of teachings, or "all dharmas agree on the one point," with the one point being a direct remedy for ego-clinging.

In this special context of mind training, we are presented with methods for diminishing and eradicating the tendency of ego-clinging. First we learn how to develop absolute bodhichitta, which is the understanding of emptiness that directly realizes that the personal identity is empty. Some kind of method is required when we resolve to achieve enlightenment. According to the advice Atisha received from Jowo Serlingpa, "Planting the seed of bodhichitta does not grow well if the soil is too clean. It grows much better in soil that is dirty and fertilized." This means that if we are considering whether there is an ego or not, we can say that the impure way of thinking that there is a self can be more conducive for giving rise to bodhichitta than the thought that there is no personal self. Therefore, in the mind training of relative bodhichitta, the main part of the practice here, we accept that there is a personal self. The reason we do that is to make it easier to give up self-cherishing and to regard others as more important than ourselves. Also in sending and taking practice we assume there is a self and there is another we are sending and taking to. The purpose of sending and taking is to reduce self-cherishing and to increase cherishing others. In this way, whether we are training in absolute or relative bodhichitta, the purpose is to decrease ego-clinging. So all three vehicles agree with one another at one point.

In the context of this training, "The Buddha's dharma converges on a single point," our evaluation of whether we are improving in our practice or not are the questions: "Is our level of self-cherishing decreasing? Is treasuring others over ourselves increasing? Is there any progress there?" This is how we keep track of progress in our practice.

B. Relying on Yourself as a Measure of Mind Training

20. Of the two witnesses, attend to the principal one.

The second way to tell whether the mind training is working is the instruction which says, "Of the two witnesses, attend to the principal one." If we are wondering whether we are good dharma practitioners or not, there are actually two possible witnesses: ourselves and others. For instance, other practitioners and friends can look at us and have an opinion of whether we are good people or not. Yet they can only see our outward behavior; they cannot really look inside our mind. So the other judge, which is our own mind, is more profound because we can see into our mind. Others can see that we are doing something which appears good to them, but only we ourselves know whether our motivation and intention are good or not. Therefore, between these two witnesses the more important one is oneself. If we can look at our behavior, not be ashamed, and know it is faultless, then that is the more important judge.

There is one more aspect to how we should evaluate progress: it is best if both witnesses were to agree that we have perfected the training. We are trying to give up self-cherishing and to treat others as more important than ourselves. Even if we are not trying our best, just thinking, "It would be good if I could" is also fine. Even if we are not feeling that way, just the attitude that thinks the teachings on mind training are "really precious teachings and I hope one day to get into them" is also fine. In this way, it is beneficial to evaluate whether or not we have the right attitude and the noble intention of diminishing self-cherishing and cherishing others as higher.

C. State of Mind as a Measure of Mind Training

21. At all times, rely only on a joyful mind.

Another way to evaluate our practice is to check our mind to see what kind of state it is in. This will also tell us how well our practice is going. For instance, when illness, accidents, or tragedies happen and we become frightened about them to the extent that depression sets in, our mind training practice isn't working. If these conditions always get the better of us, then the practice is ineffective. Instead of this happening, when negative circumstances occur, we can use our mind training. These obstacles then become like friends of mind training, and we can be happy about them. It is another measure that our mind training practice is working. If something negative happens and we think that we can't bear such suffering, then our practice is not working. But if negative things happen and we instead instantly think, "So many people have catastrophes like this. I wish that I could take on all of their suffering as well," then we know that whatever happens becomes an aid to our mind training. In this way, our mind is always in a happy state because we are able to use whatever arises as part of our practice.

The real measurement for mind training is to be found in the instruction: "At all times, rely only on a joyful mind." This has to do with the degree to which we have succeeded in refusing self-cherishing because as long as there is the tendency to refer to "me" as being so important, then there is selfish hope and fear. By hope we mean thinking, "I hope such and such will happen. If it doesn't, I will be disappointed." By fear we mean, "I have this really nice thing or situation, I am afraid I might lose it." We are preoccupied with trying to get what we want, trying to arrange the circumstances for our happiness. This selfish activity is accompanied by worry about what we don't want. We are concerned that an undesirable situation might happen; when it does, we will become upset and unhappy.

D. Staying on Guard

22. If you can practice even when distracted, you are well trained.

Another way to evaluate progress in mind training is that we spontaneously think of others, even when we are not consciously working with our practice. So when events arise and we aren't consciously thinking of our practice, instead of getting flustered and forgetting our intention, our natural reaction is bodhichitta, thinking of others. If our first, spontaneous thought shows that we are not giving preference to ourselves, then this is a sign that even though we are distracted, our practice is working.

When we are practicing mind training and we have some results of the practice, the tendency to become conceited may arise, "I am special now. I got somewhere through the practice. This is good enough for me." Don't be too happy about having some results because we need to reach complete enlightenment and be capable of helping each and every living being. Until we are capable of helping every being reach liberation, we have not reached our goal. There is no reason to congratulate ourselves too early and be inflated with pride just because we have some signs of practice.

Another type of thought can arise: "Okay, I am practicing mind training but there is not much of a result." We may become disappointed and discouraged thinking: "I am a hopeless practitioner. I am not getting anywhere. Maybe there is no way for someone like me really to achieve this kind of practice." We may even become disheartened and give up, which is also not necessary because we have achieved one result of practice already—simply understanding the goodness of reducing self-cherishing and valuing mind training. Understanding this is already a sign of good mind training and we may be able to improve upon that by carrying on without being disheartened.

As we apply ourselves to this training, we train our mind. It is not a matter of looking like a good practitioner; rather it has to do with putting our heart into it. As the Buddha taught, our goal is to thoroughly train our mind. It is not a matter of being successful, but of trying our best. So whether we have perfected mind training or not or whether we are trying to become fully enlightened, it is fine. We may not have totally trained our own mind yet, but we are moving in that direction, which is good.

chapter seven

THE COMMITMENTS OF MIND TRAINING

VI. COMMITMENTS OF MIND TRAINING

THIS SECTION DEALS WITH THE commitments of mind training. "Commitment" here means the promises that we make with this mind training. Basically, we promise to work for the benefit of all other beings. That promise should not be broken: we should work for the benefit of others and remember that in all our activities.

The word "commitment" (Skt. *samaya*, Tib. *damtsig*) is often regarded as something extremely dangerous and risky. Commitment is definitely something you need to observe, respect, and adhere to, but you need not fear it. A commitment is given by the teacher to insure that disciples follow the right course, avoiding hindrances and side-tracks, to proceed in a way that is good and beneficial. It is the teacher's responsibility to make sure of that and the word *commitment* refers to this. When the disciple makes up his or her mind to follow a certain course, a mental pledge to do so is made. Having committed themselves to practice in a certain way, then they should follow that, otherwise what's the point? There is no need to make a commitment if you are not going to follow it. The purpose of making the commitment is to make sure that you move in the right direction, avoiding obstacles and progressing along the path.

The commitments of mind training have eighteen instructions that are discussed below.

A. THREE GENERAL PRINCIPLES

Three general principles define the making of commitments: not to break promises; not to act in a pretentious manner; and not to be one-sided.

23. *Always train in the three basic principles.*

The first basic principle is not to break the promise to work for the benefit of others. To do this we often take extra vows, such as the individual liberation vows, the bodhisattva vows, and the tantric vows.[21] Whichever vows we have taken, they should not be broken.

The basic principle of mind training is to make the commitment to try our best to diminish selfishness and to promote loving-kindness, compassion, and bodhichitta. What happens when we try our best? We may be successful or not. Our situation may change from time to time. Sometimes our tendency to be selfish diminishes and sometimes it swells again. Sometimes we are compassionate and caring for others, at other times we are not. Does this mean we are in conflict with the basic commitment? Have we violated or broken our samaya with mind training? No. Success is not the measurement of whether we are in harmony with the commitment but whether we keep up our efforts or not. For example, if we totally turn our back on the practice and say, "This just doesn't work! Ego-clinging is a part of me and there is nothing I can do about it. Being selfish is how I am," then we have broken our commitment. Or if we insist, "There is no way I can be more kind and compassionate and develop bodhichitta. It is something I am not cut out to do," the commitment is broken. If we are not that good at arousing bodhichitta, it doesn't mean we have broken our commitment, but rather that we need to try a little harder. As long as we have the attitude, "I will try my best to reduce self-cherishing. I will try my best to promote loving-kindness, compassion, and bodhichitta," then we are still in harmony with the commitment and it remains unbroken.

The second basic principle is not to act in a pretentious way. We may have the intention of showing others that we are really practicing mind training and have no attachment to self. As a result, we might start doing outrageous things like not caring for our body or clothes, looking like a beggar, or acting like a madman. This is what is meant by "acting outrageously." If our motive is to make others think, "Oh, this person has perfected some kind of great dharma," then that motive is impure and should be avoided. Acting crazy for no good reason only calls attention to us.

"Don't resort to pretentiousness." means don't put on a show of having perfected mind training, of not being selfish any longer. It is not like refusing to take medicine because you have stopped caring, but reflects more on our attitude towards others, who might get a wrong impression. Being pretentious is rude and unnecessary. The instruction is: Don't do that.

The third basic principal is "Do not be partial or biased." For instance, we might sometimes have patience with the negativities of human beings, but then we are impatient with the harm caused by non-humans. Or maybe we can stand it when animals cause us some kind of harm, but we can't stand the same treatment from humans. Or sometimes we have great patience with our friends, but none with strangers or people who don't like us. Then again, we may have patience for all of these, but none when we become sick. So again, this is what is meant be being "one-sided." We should be able to bear all, and we should have an attitude of equanimity towards every situation and type of being. We should not divide our loving-kindness and compassion so that they are directed towards some and not others. Or when things are going well and there are no problems, we feel very compassionate, but when things go wrong, it disappears. We should not have biased or partial compassion.

B. Specific Principles

24. Change your attitude and be natural.

The fourth point, "Change your attitude and be natural," has two parts. Normally, we are selfish and disregard the importance of others. Changing that means being unselfish and caring. The second part is acting naturally, i.e., not being conceited about unselfishness, about diminishing self-importance, and regarding others as more important. All this does not mean that we are special or superior to others. Or we may begin to criticize those who do not follow this pattern of behavior. Instead of criticizing them and putting on airs about our practice, we should be kinder to them. The meaning of acting naturally is being equal to and in harmony with anyone you meet. We should not deliberately act differently from them, but be naturally, even though our attitude has changed.

25. Don't speak ill of others' shortcomings.

The fifth point is that we should not talk about others' weaknesses. This mainly has to do with how we communicate. When we do so, our words should be nice and not unpleasant, the main point here. Others' business has to do with how they look, how they speak, with their attitude and whether they are rich or not. We may think that there is something wrong in some of these areas, but that doesn't mean we have to speak about it. In terms of dharma practice, something may be lacking but it doesn't mean it is our job to point this out to everyone. There is another point here, which has to do with our motivation. If we really have a good heart and are sure that others will change by what we say, then it is a different matter. If we say it nicely, that's okay. But if it is said out of ill-will, rivalry, spite or other negative emotions, then it belongs to talking about others' weaknesses, which should be avoided.

We should not engage in conversations about others' faults. We don't point out faults in people who have physical deficiencies such as lameness or blindness, or mental deficiencies such as stupidity.

Likewise, we don't point out dharma faults in others, such as their being lazy and not practicing, or their breaking their vows. In other words, we don't say harmful things about others. Rather, with a smile we should speak in a very gentle and loving manner, in a way that makes sense and is pleasing to them.

26. Don't ponder the affairs of others.

The previous instruction dealt with the way we act, while this instruction concerns motivation. If we have faults, we need to think about them and be concerned about them; otherwise, the faults will only increase and grow stronger. So we need to look at our faults because nobody else can do that for us. But when it comes to others' faults, we don't need to look for them, especially those of our dharma friends and other dharma practitioners. Of course, they are going to have faults and that is something which they themselves will have to deal with. It is their own karma, so there is absolutely no point in our doing it for them. In fact, getting involved in others' faults can only bring harm. We can't fix or do anything about the faults others possess. They have to deal with their own problems. If they are lazy, they may be doing the best they can. Most people who have entered the dharma do try. They may have large obstacles, but they do the best they can. For us to search for their faults and point them out doesn't make any sense at all and doesn't do any good. We need only to examine our own faults.

In other words, we may spend a lot of attention trying to figure out what others are doing and whether it is right or wrong. Because we bring such thoughts into our mind, sooner or later it becomes a matter of speech, the fifth instruction. Here, we are just pondering others' affairs and that is unnecessary. Rather, it is better simply to respect others and trust that they are probably doing their best, doing what they consider right. Afterwards, we work with becoming used to this view. If, out of a good heart, we see faults then, of course, it is all right to see if it is possible to mend them.

When we begin to work on ourselves by examining our faults we then:

27. Work with the stronger afflictions first.

When we examine our own faults, we see that we have many afflictions or disturbing emotions. The first thing to do is determine which disturbing emotion we have the most trouble with. Once we recognize that, then we need to work on it because it is our special weak point. We should concentrate all of our practice on our strongest disturbing emotion and work on that one first.

In the beginning, we are trying to deal with the negative patterns of how we speak, then with our mental attitude which is more difficult. Some disturbing emotions are dominant in our stream of being, so we need to determine what emotion haunts us. Is it anger we are always preoccupied with? Or is it rivalry? Is it attachment? Once we identify the emotion, we can try to work on it. For example, while doing prostrations we can make up our mind, "All right. I am doing prostrations, but it is primarily to overcome the particular emotion of anger or attachment." When we are doing the Vajrasattva meditation with nectar pouring into us, we can imagine that a specific negative emotion is being purified. Dealing with it in this way, we can overcome our strongest negative emotion.

After identifying our greatest fault and beginning to work on it, we then:

28. Send away any hope for results.

Giving up hope has to do with thinking that we are gaining some nice results from mind training: we are able to be more kind and compassionate to others, less selfish and so forth. But then, we may hold in the back of our mind that if we are good, people will be nice in return. We have some expectation of being rewarded for being a good person and having a good heart. Or we could expect, "As I become a better practitioner, others will know me for being so. They will respect me, and I will become important in some way." Or maybe we think about good results later on. For example, "I will get something important out of this at some point." Of course, it is not the case that we won't; there is a definite consequence of practice that ripens as a result. In the context of mind training, we give up all hope for results.

This connects with the next instruction:

29. Avoid poisonous food.

To tame our disturbing emotions, we try to help others. But if all our efforts do not result in decreasing our ego, then no matter how much virtue we have practiced, it is like eating food that is poisoned. The result of eliminating the disturbing emotions must be that self-clinging decreases. If we are doing mind training with the hope of benefiting ourselves, then it is as if that virtue were poisoned.

This instruction is obviously a metaphor. We all eat, but if there is poison in the food, it is harmful. In the same way, we need to progress on the spiritual path and do what is good and meaningful, but if a selfish attitude is mixed with that, then the root cause of samsara (of clinging to a personal identity and ego) is not totally eradicated because there is some poison mixed with practice. We should try to overcome that.

The next instruction is difficult to translate into English. There are several completely different translations of it, such as, "Don't rely on our natural tendency," but we render it as:

30. Don't be so constant.

In our life, we are quite consistent in our actions: if somebody is very good to us, we are kind in return, whereas if somebody harms us, then we try to take revenge. That is what "consistency" means here. The instruction is suggesting that we act in the opposite way from a worldly person: If somebody harms us, we need to respond with kindness, not to exact revenge: we seek to benefit them not to harm them.

Consistency is usually a good quality and describes someone who has a good character continuously and is not flaky, someone who still has integrity through many years, and a noble heart. It is good to have consistency, but here it means something else: It has to do with how we usually are. Should we continue sticking to the way we usually are, to the tendency to be selfish, and to regard ourselves as really important? No. That is not necessary, which is what is meant in this verse.

31. *Don't get riled by critical remarks.*

The general instruction is not to talk about others' weak points and not to concern ourselves with their affairs. This instruction is more specific in that it says not to return cutting remarks. If somebody says something bad about us, we don't get upset and say something sarcastic or cutting in return.

32. *Don't lie in ambush.*

If someone has hurt us in some way, we usually think, "However long it takes, I'm going to wait until I have a chance to get back at you. One day that chance will come and then I'm going to get you." That is what is meant by waiting in ambush. The teaching is obviously to just let the hurt go.

33. *Don't strike at weak points.*

This instruction means that even if we see something terribly wrong with someone, we don't point it out to them or hurt them in some way. Also, if negative non-human beings[22] are doing us some kind of harm, we don't do a special practice to harm them in return. In other words, even though we see that someone has a great fault, we don't do something to hurt them.

This instruction means that we speak pleasantly to someone, but actually we have unpleasant thoughts about them and so there is deceit hiding in our words. This instruction is a little different from the instruction, "Don't disparage others," in that it is more deceitful and thus more hateful.

34. Don't transfer a dzo's burden onto an ox.

A *dzo* is half yak and half cow; possibly from a male yak and female cow, or the other way around, from a female yak called *dri* and a bull. The offspring is very strong and able to carry a larger load than an ox, but it is also much more expensive because it can work harder and can carry a heavier load. This instruction means that everyone should carry the burden appropriate to him or her. If you take the dzo's load and put it on the ox, the ox will not be able to carry it for very long. So, if we have an unpleasant task which we are supposed to do, or we have some fault that is our own, we shouldn't expect someone else to take care of it. We have to address it ourselves. We cannot carry each other's burdens.

"Don't transfer a dzo's burden to an ox" has another meaning. It could also be that one thinks that the dzo is more valuable and therefore thinks, "I don't want to hurt it by overloading it, so I would rather have the ox carry the load in order to protect my dzo." That is the meaning here. When something goes wrong, we want to protect someone, probably oneself, right? In other words, we point our finger at someone else, saying, "He/she did it!" We pass the blame away from ourselves so the idea here is: Don't pass the blame.

35. Don't aim to be the fastest.

It is human nature that if we have something good, we will crave something yet better. If something is done on time, we want to do it even quicker. If everybody has something we already have, we want ours even bigger or nicer. That's why we are taught, "Don't aim to be the fastest."

When three people join in a race, the aim is to be the first. The attitude each has is, "I can win." We can hold this kind of attitude when we do other things, like dharma studies. We want to be the best, the winner. That is not what is called a noble heart, which should be, "I will try my best, but I am also happy when others are successful. It is not necessary for me to be better than they are."

36. Don't act with a twist.

The literal meaning in Tibetan of this instruction is that we don't undertake hardships motivated by a calculated intent. Of course, it is nice to go to trouble for others, to be willing to suffer so that others are happy, but if our motivation is to help ourselves so that in the end we win material things or receive acclaim from others then we are acting with a hidden motivation.

We might say, "Okay, I agree you won in this case," with the hidden intent that it is ultimately we who will prevail. Or we might give something to somebody, not out of generosity, but because we hope to get something from them later on. This is the wrong motivation.

37. Don't turn gods into demons.

Suppose we are practicing mind training and things are going very well. We may then develop pride in our accomplishments and think, "Oh, I did so well at this mind training that now I'm really a great practitioner." Or we might develop envy for others who are progressing much more rapidly than we are. In both these cases we are making a god into a demon. In this analogy, the mind training practice, which goes well for us or for someone else, is like a god. If this accomplishment creates a negative emotion such as pride, then it is like a demon.

"Don't make a god into a demon," means don't degrade the practice of mind training. We are trying to cultivate the noble heart of bodhichitta, but then we may become proud of ourselves because of being a bodhisattva and think we are special and superior to others who are not doing so. This is called "degrading one's purity," in the sense that it hardens our sensitivity so that we don't really care for others and are more inclined to be rude. That is called "turning a god into a demon," or "degrading the practice."

38. Don't seek others' pain as the limbs of your happiness.

This means that even though we wish well for everyone, there is some kind of negative undertone in it. For instance, wishing for our own happiness, we might wish that something bad happens to somebody else. We shouldn't do that. We may think that if our friend had some misfortune befall him, then it will show us in a better light. This would be seeking another's pain as a component of our own happiness. Even the thought, "If my enemy dies, then it is good for me," is seeking pain as a component of one's own happiness and it is wrong.

We shouldn't rejoice in others' misfortune. For instance, if there is someone causing us trouble, of course, it would be much better for us if they stopped. If they suddenly die or experience a disaster, it doesn't mean we may rejoice and comment, "Hey, great!" That would be called seeking others' pain as a limb of our own happiness.

These are the commitments of mind training. The main point of the commitment here is to try our best. If we are successful, fine; if not, continue trying.

Questions

Question: This is regarding the instruction about not concerning yourself with the affairs of others. In many American Buddhist communities, the members have not paid attention when bad things were happening within the community, and so people were hurt. Not becoming involved seems to go against the spirit of the mind training practice. If you watch something happen that will damage others, yet you refuse to become involved, isn't this violating the whole spirit of the teaching?

Rinpoche: The instruction doesn't mean that we should let any kind of harm just happen. What this particular instruction is talking about is what most people usually do: They look for people's faults when there is no need to look for them. Of course, in a situation where you clearly see that somebody is doing something very harmful to you or others, then it is your responsibility to stop them if you can.

If someone is going to harm you, then you can talk to them and say, "Look, if you do this, then it is bad in a worldly sense and it is bad in a dharma sense." If you are able to stop them, that is very good. Likewise, if they are doing something harmful to someone else and you can, by explaining the negative results of these actions, prevent them from engaging in the bad action, then it is very beneficial. In fact, mind training suggests that you must do that. This instruction talks about the times when we search out others' faults for no reason at all.

Question: In everyday life, there are situations where people are really driving you crazy. You said we should look at them smilingly and pretend. That means I wouldn't be honest. If somebody repeatedly does something that gets on my nerves, like using my soap, then after three years I say, "Stop now!"
Rinpoche: If it is not a big thing and you are able just to be patient, then it is good to practice patience. However, if it is something that isn't big but continually annoying to you and you are not able to be patient about it, you can, in a skillful manner without being angry and yelling, say, "This is annoying me." Deal with it in a skillful manner.

Question: Is there a recommendation against being socially active in a community, to bring a positive change to the community from the point of view of practice? Does becoming involved with people in that way contradict what some of the instructions indicate?
Rinpoche: The intention is always to help others, and that should be done in whatever way you can. But whether you are doing it effectively or not depends upon your state of mind. So that is why all these teachings talk so much about taming your mind. If your mind is in the right place, then any help you may give will arise spontaneously. You won't even need to think, "Oh, I should help that person!" It happens automatically. But if you haven't worked with your mind and you go out trying to help people, it might be that without your knowing it there is some other kind of motivation, fault, or lack of skillful means at play. For example, you might suddenly, in the middle

of all your efforts, become completely exhausted and think, "I just cannot do this any more." Or you might feel unconsciously proud over being helpful, having the motivation of wanting something in return. So wisdom and skill have to go together. We can make a distinction: What is more important? Helping others or taming our own mind? While ultimately the goal is to help others, the first thing to do is to tame our own mind so that we are able to help others effectively.

Question: My question is: How do we know when an emotion is negative? Anger seems very obvious, but I think there are more subtle things like fear or other emotions like that. My second question is whether the Vajrasattva practice is appropriate for all negative emotions?

Rinpoche: If an emotion is directly harmful to others or indirectly, or implicitly harmful to others, then it is called "negative." If it is beneficial either directly or indirectly, then it is called "positive." Okay?

Does the Vajrasattva practice eliminate negative emotions? No, it cannot totally eliminate negative emotions but this practice can lessen the intensity of the negative emotions.

chapter eight

GUIDELINES FOR MIND TRAINING

VII. GUIDELINES OF MIND TRAINING

THE FINAL SECTION OF MIND training deals with advice on mind training which is given through twenty-one instructions. These are divided into two sections: what we should reject and what we should adopt.

A. WHAT TO REJECT

39. All practices should be done with one intention.

Practice here includes the training of meditation in the post-meditation state: how to practice while eating, while walking, while sitting, while lying down, while talking to others, and so forth. In other words, whatever activities we do, there is one way to focus, one way to practice. In this particular context of mind training, i.e., training our attitude of bodhichitta, it means being benevolent, and this implies never parting from the good-will of wanting to benefit others in all that we do, whether we are able to bring all living beings into our focus or only a few. This is the first guideline: "All practices should be done with one intention."

40. One practice corrects everything.

Whenever anything bad happens to us such as being hurt by others, having a serious accident, seeing our disturbing emotions increase greatly, or losing our desire to meditate, we should think about how many living beings in the world have the similar misfortunes, and how painful it is for them. We should wish that on top of our own suffering, we could take on the suffering of all others. This is the antidote to whatever misfortune befalls us.

The next instruction tells us how to deal with these misfortunes:

41. At the start and the finish, an activity to be done.

The third point has to do with how we conduct ourselves on a daily basis. The start is our first thought for the day, when we wake up in the morning. We should make up our mind: "This is a new day. How am I going to use it in practice, not only for absolute but also relative bodhichitta? I will try my best with body, speech and mind to live in accordance with these principles in how I behave, in how I eat—in my attitude towards everything." Then we go about our daily activities and at the end of the day, while in bed, we think: "This morning I made up my mind to follow bodhichitta. How well did I do in my physical actions and behavior? How well did I do with my speech to others? Did I do it with the bodhisattva principle? How well have I kept the commitment I made this morning?" If I notice that I did quite fine, then I can rejoice and add: "It was good. I will continue in this same way the next days as well." If I noticed that I was not that great, then I can say, "This wasn't a good day. I will try to do better in the future." Then we go to sleep. So, there is one way to begin the day and another way to conclude it, what is meant by "At the start and finish, an activity to be done."

42. Whichever of the two occurs, be patient.

To simplify, we can say that there are only two outcomes to any situation: positive or negative. If bad things happen, we should not blame anyone else: it is our own misfortune coming from our own karma. Therefore, we should think that the only thing to do about this unfortunate situation is to clear up all non-virtuous karma and pray that it may not happen to other beings as well. If good things happen, then we should not become careless or lazy, but wish that these good things happen to others. Also, whatever good happens, such as wealth, power, or influence, should be turned to some positive use.

If things were always pleasant and we were successful and experienced good circumstances, it is quite likely that we would become too attached to that and expect that everything would be fine. Because of being too fond of having a good time and enjoying ourselves, it is quite likely that we would forget about our concern for other beings and become insensitive. If things always go wrong and we continuously have problems, it is quite likely that we will get caught up in that and worry about ourselves too much. The instructions here are to be willing to be patient with whatever happens, whether good or bad times.

Whatever happens we should:

43. Maintain these two, even at the risk of your life.

There is a phrase in Tibetan which is "higher than you would your own life." Is there anything we hold more dear than our life? When it is lost, we cannot continue, so it is most precious to us. Yet, for a practitioner of mind training, there is something more precious, and that is what to adopt and what to avoid. This means we should adopt what is virtuous and avoid what is non-virtuous. We should realize that discriminating between what is good and what is evil is actually more important than our own life.

We should always try to maintain all of our Vajrayana vows (Skt. *samaya*) and particularly the vows of the mind training. The final instruction concerns disturbing emotions:

44. Train in the three difficult points.

To eliminate disturbing emotions there are three things we can do. The first is to recognize a disturbing emotion when it arises. The second is to turn it back, which means to employ the remedy very forcefully. Even though we have recognized the disturbing emotions and have employed the remedy to eliminate them, we must perform the third activity, which is to cut them off completely. This means ridding ourselves of them altogether, which is the most difficult activity of the three because it requires a great deal of diligence and mindfulness. Up to now, the points have dealt with what needed to be abandoned. Next are instructions concerning what we should adopt.

B. WHAT TO ADOPT

There are three preliminary conditions or causes for a successful dharma practice:

45. Take up the three main causes.

These three causes are: (a) relying on an authentic teacher; (b) settling our mind very firmly in the dharma so that it becomes workable; and (c) having the necessary materials to practice, such as clothes, food, implements, and time. We must work to have all these circumstances come together for us. This has to do with not turning away from the seeds mentioned.

The first cause is a genuine spiritual teacher who is realized. We should not have trust in someone who acts contrary to the spiritual teachings. Let's say we have met someone who teaches something that is correct, invaluable, and worthy. This essential trust insures that we can practice. If we don't trust the teachings and the teacher, then how can we carry through with the instructions? So that sense of trust is something to keep, and we should not let it slip away.

The second cause is to have enthusiasm for mind training, delight in practicing and applying the instructions, having understood their value, and, finally, being happy to continue. The third cause is not to turn away from mind training itself, not to forget what is to be avoided and what is to be adopted. When this is done:

46. Pay attention that these three things do not diminish.

There are three things that we should not let diminish in power. First, because the lama is the root of all virtues, we should not let our trust for him diminish. Second, because mind training teachings are essential to the Mahayana, we should not let our joy and delight in practicing these teachings diminish. Finally, we should not let any of our vows diminish.

47. Keep the three inseparable.

We should also make sure that virtuous activity is inseparable from body, speech, and mind. Next, we should:

48. Train impartially in all areas; deep, pervasive, and constant training is crucial.

Being impartial is how we train in loving-kindness and compassion: we don't favor those who deserve our love and compassion or turn our backs on others. Rather, we make no distinctions in being kind and compassionate. It is said we should be impartial in all areas of our practice and not limit ourselves. The second aspect is to make this pervasive: there is no barrier or limitation to any area of our training in how we regard others. We train totally to embrace everyone. It also means that we do not look outside, but rather at our own hearts and minds. Whenever it is difficult to be loving and kind, we work to overcome that barrier. When we feel like holding back our compassion, we train to overcome this withdrawal.

We should not just practice mind training and compassion towards one living being while overlooking another. Mind training and bodhichitta should apply to all human and non-human beings without exception. This instruction extends into the next:

49. Always meditate on what aggravates you.

When we have an opponent or someone we don't like, it is harder to feel love and compassion. When someone tries to hurt us emotionally or physically, this is an opportunity to be extra loving and kind to that person. There are also those who are not grateful. We have been kind to them, but they turn against us or do not appreciate what we have done. For these people in particular, there is the opportunity to train by having good feelings towards them.

This instruction to practice training with the most difficult persons and circumstances means we should begin practice with those individuals who are especially hateful to us, those who try to harm and fight with us, and with those who harm us even when we have no bad feelings towards them. For these difficult individuals, we should make an extra effort and try to be especially skillful in our mind training.

50. Don't be swayed by outer circumstances.

When we feel very happy, our health is good, and everything seems to be going well, we feel that we can practice, whereas when we are feeling ill and things are going poorly, we think that we cannot practice. This is relying on external conditions to determine if we will practice or not. The instruction, therefore, means that whether we are feeling well or not, whether we are healthy or not, whether we have money or not, whether people are kind to us or not, whether we have all the proper conditions for practicing or not, we should still practice. Not only do we not rely on external conditions but:

51. This time practice what is most important.

This time we have attained a precious human birth and come into contact with the dharma, so we have the most important elements necessary to practice. Out of all the things we can do with our life, practice is the most important because it alone has a lasting benefit. The next instruction is:

52. Don't make mistakes.

Sometimes we show great diligence and patience in our worldly affairs, but we do not show the same patience and diligence in our dharma practice. If we are like that, then we have "mistaken patience" and "mistaken diligence." In other words, we should not apply good qualities to an incorrect object.

In our practice, we are trying to develop the qualities of trust, devotion, kindness, and compassion. It is possible to place our trust in someone who is not trustworthy or to feel sorry for those who undertake hardships in order to practice the dharma. Rather, we should feel sorry for people who are confused and get emotionally carried away. So, take care not to be mistaken in these ways.

In addition we are told:

53. Don't fluctuate.

Sometimes we have great faith and devotion, and sometimes we don't. Sometimes we have great energy and diligence and sometimes we don't. Sometimes we really believe in the teachings and sometimes we don't. We shouldn't fluctuate like this: we should be single-minded and simply practice. In addition to not applying our diligence in the wrong way and oscillating:

54. Train with your whole heart.

This means to be completely positive that what we want to do is to practice and not become distracted by other activities. In other words, we must stay single-minded about the practice. Training wholeheartedly has the sense of not being timid or hesitant about practicing because the practice seems too vast and difficult. "With your whole heart" means acting courageously, being brave, and taking the step. The kind of bravery needed is to think, "I can do this." Even if we haven't been able to succeed, we still have the courageous attitude. That is important.

An element of single-mindedness is to:

55. Free yourself through examination and analysis.

This means we should free ourselves from disturbing emotions, which we can do by continually examining our mind. We ask ourselves: "Has a disturbing emotion come up? Have I managed to get rid of it?" and so on, always being very conscious of what is going on in our mind.

When we have practiced, we may at some point get the feeling, "This practice is going quite well. I am succeeding and am not so selfish anymore. I also feel more kind and compassionate and caring." This may be true, but it doesn't mean that we should just rest on our laurels, thinking, "Now everything is fine." We should put it to the test to see whether or not it is really true or only an impression we have. When it becomes most evident is when we are in a tight and difficult situation because then we can see how our reaction is. Do we react immediately with kindness and compassion? If we behave very nicely in difficult situations, then it is okay. Then we can agree, "Yes, I have really progressed." If we haven't, then we will see, "Oh! It was just an impression I had. I really need to try harder and continue the training."

56. Don't make a big deal about it.

There are two parts to this instruction: the first is to avoid thinking, "Oh, I was so kind to that person." Or, "Oh, I practice so well. I try so hard. I'm so good." The second is to avoid expecting appreciation for our good works. For instance, we might think, "I am so kind to that person that he should be kind to me." If we have such expectations, then our practice won't go well. Related closely to this is:

57. Don't let being irritated tie you up.

If someone harms us, whether they intended it or not, we should not think, "Well, they did this to me, so I will never help them again." This is the meaning of being overly sensitive and irritable.

It is human nature to be ill-humored when something annoying happens. But a practitioner of mind training will try not to react with anger. Instead, a practitioner tries to get to the point where he or she does not immediately react with anger.

Closely related to this instruction is:

58. Don't overreact.

If bad things happen, we should not get overly upset or depressed; if good things happen, we should not get overly excited and happy. The idea is to be very even-tempered. Whatever happens, good or bad, we should stay on an even keel.

59. Don't expect a standing ovation.

The final instruction means not to expect thanks, congratulations, or fame from the activity of helping others. If we do something good for someone, we should not wait for them to thank us, or expect that we might become admired or famous. We shouldn't expect anything like this.

This last instruction "Don't expect a standing ovation," may sound like the instruction, "Don't make a big deal about it," and in some ways they are similar. One is being kind in the hope of being treated nicely in return. Here, it is more thinking of our reputation and hoping to be spoken of nicely.

All twenty-one points are about the same principle—having a good heart, a good intention, or a noble resolve. The reason why there are so many instructions in this section is that sometimes our good heart may be a little rusty, in need of a little cleaning in certain situations. Sometimes we think: "It doesn't really matter. I'll do this anyway." Well, in fact it does matter. That is the reason why twenty-one points are listed here, so that we see different situations: how not to be pretentious, not to be irritable, not to fluctuate, not to expect thanks, etc. In these areas we need to improve a bit so that our good heart can be really clean and pure.

Even though this completes the teaching of the mind training, I would like to add something on how these teachings come to our Kagyu lineage. In this lineage, Gampopa received the Mahamudra instructions from Milarepa, who received them from Marpa. Gampopa also received the mind training lineage from Atisha and he combined the two lineages. To practice both of these instructions is very significant. Mahamudra is a subtle and profound teaching, and if you are able to realize it, you can cut off all disturbing emotions and self-clinging at the root. But sometimes this alone doesn't work. It is said that if the view is too high for a practitioner's existing level— if we don't enter the path in the proper way—we end up with more disturbing emotions, in particular pride and jealousy. If this happens, we need to practice mind training, which is like medicine for the mind when the emotions get strong. The opposite can also happen. We may be practicing mind training, but it doesn't include enough of the ultimate view. Then we should practice the Mahamudra teachings to develop a higher view.

There are also certain situations in which the Mahamudra teachings might be easier to practice. For instance, they are good to do in retreat and will help us progress easily. But at other times, when we are living in the world and associating with other people, unfortunate circumstances can arise, at which time mind training may be easier. It is therefore important to practice both.

The Conclusion

This essential elixir of instruction,
Transforming the five kinds of degeneration
Into the path of awakening,
Is a transmission from Serlingpa.

Having awakened the karmic energy of previous
    training,
I was moved by deep devotion;
Therefore, ignoring suffering and criticism,
I sought out instruction on how to subdue ego-fixation.
Now when I die, I'll have no regret.

It is said that we live in degenerate times in which many things have declined, our life span and pure views. On the other hand, there is an increase in the number of material objects and situations giving rise to the disturbing emotions, such as aggression, desire, attachment, and jealousy. Rather than thinking of these situations as misfortunes, we should think of them as something that helps us on the path of dharma. These mind training instructions allow us to continue with whatever happens on the path to enlightenment. Because of them, the darkness of our time is said to be like *healing nectar* (Skt. *amrita*). These teachings are also very precious because they are from the lineage of Guru Serlingpa.

This concludes *The Seven Points of Mind Training*. These two verses at the end explain the goodness and value of these teachings. It is said that we live in a dark age, characterized by five kinds of degenerations: the level of philosophical views degenerates; the afflicting emotions increase; life spans shorten, our quality of life declines; and living beings decline physically and mentally. In short, there is a lot of negativity during the times in which we live. Even though the five degenerations increase, it is possible to train in the path of enlightenment at these times. And through these instructions on mind training, which are like the nectar of immortality, negativities can subside. These instructions are like precious amrita. Where do they come from? They were handed down through the lineage from Suvarnadvipa, meaning the "Master from Sumatra on the Golden Continent."

The second verse demonstrates the greatness of these instructions. The author, Chekawa Yeshe Dorje, tells how he himself went about receiving the teachings, and what happened to him. He writes that it must be due to the awakening of his training in a previous life that he could have trust and a connection with such a teaching, because he did not shun any hardships to receive them. He further states that he disregarded slander and disparagement by others and still managed to receive and also practice these teachings on mind training. What happened? He gained a confidence, ease, and peace of mind to the extent that he says in the last sentence, "Now, when I die, I'll have no regret." In other words, even at the time of death he has nothing to fear; he is completely confident and has total peace of mind. Implicit here is an injunction to the readers and to future disciples of mind training to disregard difficulties they may have to experience in receiving these teachings and undergoing the training. In this way, they will also gain confidence and fearlessness even at the time of death.

THE ROOT TEXT OF THE SEVEN POINTS OF MIND TRAINING

translated by

Michele Martin

THE SEVEN POINTS OF MIND TRAINING IN THE MAHAYANA

I. PRELIMINARIES: A BASIS FOR DHARMA PRACTICE

1. First, train in the preliminaries

II. THE MAIN PRACTICE, TRAINING IN BODHICHITTA

A. *Ultimate Bodhichitta*
2. Regard all phenomena as dreams.
3. Investigate the nature of unborn awareness.
4. Even the antidote is released in its ground.
5. Rest within the all-basis, the essential nature.
6. In post-meditation, regard all beings as illusions.

B. *Relative Bodhichitta*
7. Alternately practice sending and taking; these two should ride the breath.
8. Three objects, three poisons, and three roots of virtue.
9. In all your activities, train with these words.
10. Begin the sequence of sending and taking with yourself.

III. TRANSFORMING ADVERSE CONDITIONS INTO THE PATH OF AWAKENING

11. When the world is filled with negativity, transform adverse conditions into the path of awakening.

A. *Relative Bodhichitta*
12. Drive all blame into one.
13. Be grateful to everyone and everything.

B. *Ultimate Bodhichitta*
14. Seeing delusive appearances as the four kayas is the unexcelled protection emptiness gives.

C. *Special Practices*
15. The best method entails four practices.
16. Whatever you meet, instantly join it with meditation.

IV. BLENDING MIND WITH THE PRACTICE THROUGHOUT YOUR LIFE

A. *What to Do during Your Daily Life*
17. Practice the five powers, the condensed heart instructions.

B. *What To Do at Death*
18. The Mahayana instructions for transferring consciousness at death are the five powers; the way you behave matters.

V. HOW TO EVALUATE YOUR MIND TRAINING

19. All the Buddha's dharma converges on a single point.
20. Of the two witnesses, attend to the principal one.
21. At all times, rely only on a joyful mind.
22. If you can practice even when distracted, you are well trained.

VI. THE COMMITMENTS OF MIND TRAINING

23. Always train in the three basic principles.
24. Change your attitude and be natural.
25. Don't speak ill of others' shortcomings.

26. Don't ponder the affairs of others.
27. Work with the stronger afflictions first.
28. Send away any hope for results.
29. Avoid poisonous food.
30. Don't be so constant.
31. Don't get riled by critical remarks.
32. Don't lie in ambush.
33. Don't strike at weak points.
34. Don't transfer a dzo's burden onto an ox.
35. Don't aim to be the fastest.
36. Don't act with a twist.
37. Don't turn gods into demons.
38. Don't seek others' pain as the limbs of your happiness.

VII. GUIDELINES FOR MIND TRAINING

39. All practices should be done with one intention.
40. One practice corrects everything.
41. At the start and finish, an activity to be done.
42. Whichever of the two occurs, be patient.
43. Maintain these two, even at the risk of your life.
44. Train in the three difficult points.
45. Take up the three main causes.
46. Pay attention that these three things do not diminish.
47. Keep the three inseparable.
48. Train impartially in all areas; deep, pervasive, and constant training is crucial.
49. Always meditate on what aggravates you.
50. Don't be swayed by outer circumstances.
51. This time practice is central.
52. Don't make mistakes.
53. Don't fluctuate.
54. Train with your whole heart.
55. Free yourself through examination and analysis.
56. Don't make a big deal about it.

57. Don't let being irritated tie you up.
58. Don't overreact.
59. Don't expect a standing ovation.

This essential elixir of instruction,
Transforming the five kinds of degeneration
Into the path of awakening,
Is a transmission from Serlingpa.
Having awakened the karmic energy of previous training
I was moved by deep devotion;
Therefore, ignoring suffering and criticism,
I sought out instruction on how to subdue ego-fixation.
Now when I die, I'll have no regret.

These concluding verses are from Geshe Chekawa Yeshe Dorje, who wrote this text.

The translation by Michele Martin is indebted to previous versions by Traleg Rinpoche, the Nalanda Translation Committee, Ken McLeod, and B. Alan Wallace.

Notes

1. Atisha Dipamkara Shrijnana (982-1059 C.E.) was the Indian master who brought the *lojong* teachings to Tibet in 1042, when the dharma was in decline there. Atisha was the first to combine the Wisdom, Method, and Tantric Practice lineages of *lojong*, received from two Indian yogis and from his Indonesian master, Dharmakirti, (known to Tibetans as Serlingpa).

2. Atisha's two Indian gurus for the *lojong* transmission were Maitriyogi and Dharmarakshita. Historians generally place his studies with the Indonesian master, Dharmakirti (Jowo Serlingpa) between the years 1012 and 1025 CE.

3. Geshe Chekawa Yeshe Dorje (1101-1175 C.E.) was inspired by a reading of Geshe Langri Tangpa's *Eight Verses for Training the Mind* to produce his own commentary on that text, *Seven Points of Training of the Mind.* Geshe Langri Tangpa was a direct disciple of Lama Drom Tonpa, who was in turn Atisha's principal disciple.

4. For a fuller explanation of these four ordinary foundations see Thrangu Rinpoche's *The Four Foundations of Buddhist Practice.* Namo Buddha Publications, 2001.

5. Jetsun Milarepa (1052-1135 C.E.) is one of Tibet's most beloved saints in the Mahamudra tradition. He is said to have achieved enlightenment in one lifetime by virtue of the trials he endured and teachings he practiced while studying with his guru, Marpa Lotsawa.

6. The Seven-Branch Practice (Tib. *yenlag dunpa*) is a preliminary to most Vajrayana sadhanas and comprises: (1) making prostrations, (2) making offerings, (3) purifying non-virtuous habits, (4) rejoicing in the wholesome actions of others and oneself, (5) requesting the Buddhas to teach, (6) beseeching the Buddhas not to enter paranirvana, and (7) dedicating the merit.

7. Ringsel or relics are small round stones, usually about half the size of a

pea, which can spontaneously appear in an environment of religious activity and faith. For example, when holy books were burned in Tibet by the Chinese, ringsel appeared in their ashes. They also spontaneously poured out of the great stupa in Swayambhu when His Holiness the Sixteenth Karmapa visited it in 1978, as described in *Women of Wisdom* by Tsultrim Allione.

8. Solid objects that we can point to have color and shape plus a beginning, duration, and end. For example, a cup comes from clay; it is round, has a shiny glaze, and will eventually end up as molecules of clay again scattered everywhere. The argument here is that our mind does not have these characteristics. In particular, thoughts come from nowhere, dwell nowhere, and go nowhere. So the mind is said to be "empty," which is a translation of the Sanskrit word *shunyata*. This emptiness means that mind does not have a beginning or end because it can be traced through numberless lifetimes. It is this aspect of emptiness that allows mind to change. For example, it is impossible to change a cup into a horse, because both these objects have a relative physical existence, but it is not hard to change anger into love, or ignorance into knowledge, because the mind is empty. Once we have accepted that the mind is empty, then through careful logical arguments it can be established that outer phenomena, such as rocks and trees, are also empty. This is detailed in Thrangu Rinpoche's *Open Door to Emptiness*.

9. An advanced meditation particular to the Vajrayana is the direct examination of mind, often called "looking at mind." This is taught through the "pointing out instructions" in which the lama directly introduces the student to the nature of his or her mind. This technique is part of Mahamudra meditation in the Kagyu lineage and the Dzogchen meditation of the Nyingma lineage. For more details see Thrangu Rinpoche's *Essentials of Mahamudra: Looking Directly at Mind*.

10. The use of the word "nakedly" here means that one enters a very deep state of Shamatha meditation in which one examines mind without any conceptual activity. This is "looking" at mind, rather than conceptually analyzing it as one does in the analytical meditation of the Middle Way.

11. Analytical meditation is an examination of our mind in which, upon seeing a thought, we ask, "Where did that thought come from? Where is it now? And where does it go?" In resting meditation we look at mind directly without any conceptual activity and "see" what mind is like.

12. The eight consciousnesses are: the five sensory consciousnesses of sight, hearing, smell, taste, touch, and bodily sensation. The sixth consciousness is the mental consciousness; the seventh is the afflicted consciousness (the ever-present feeling of "I"); and the eighth is the ground or alaya consciousness. For a fuller explanation, see Thrangu Rinpoche's *Transcending Ego: Distinguishing Consciousness from Wisdom.*

13. The four kayas are: (1) the dharmakaya, which is dharmata, or phenomena as they are; from this manifests (2) the sambhogakaya, which is the pure realm in which solely the Mahayana vehicle is taught, and which can be recognized only by bodhisattvas; (3) the nirmanakaya in which the Buddhas manifest as ordinary beings, such as the Shakyamuni Buddha, who was born in India; and (4) the Svabhavikakaya, which is the union of these kayas.

14. Conventional wisdom is that what is inside our mind such as thoughts, dreams, and desires are "unreal" and that outside phenomena such as trees and rocks and houses are "real." Through the careful analysis of mind and also of external phenomena using the logical arguments of the Mahayana Madhyamaka school, it can be shown that mind and also external phenomena are "empty" and not real and solid. Thrangu Rinpoche has explained this extensively in other texts, such as his *Open Door to Emptiness.* A Western analogy of this reasoning is that a chair appears to be solid and real, yet a physicist will tell us that the chair is actually made of billions of atoms which are moving at incredible speeds and these atoms are so far apart that they are 99.99% space. The wood of the chair which every human (but not animal) sees as "brown" is actually just radiation of a certain frequency and the "wood" is actually composed of carbon, hydrogen, and oxygen atoms. So when the mind sees the chair as solid and real, this is actually an illusion created by the mind and not what the chair is really made of.

15. The four powers are regret for one's negative actions; the determination not to repeat those actions; antidotes to the actions (including the generation of bodhichitta and the recitation of mantras); and reliance on refuge in the Buddha, dharma, and sangha.

16. The three methods are: preparation (taking refuge and generating bodhichitta); the main part (practicing without attachment to whatever meditative experiences may arise); and the dedication of merit to the enlightenment of all beings.

17. Thrangu Rinpoche used Jamgon Kongtrul's commentary, the *Great Path of Awakening* for these teachings.

18. One religious practice to develop merit is to walk around a stupa, shrine, or other religious object in a clockwise fashion, usually while saying mantras.

19. The intermediate state, known as the *bardo* in Tibetan, is usually known in the West as the state the mind goes through immediately after death and before entering another body.

20. The Sevenfold Posture of Vairochana involves the following points: (1) legs are crossed in vajra posture (or however close we can come); (2) the hands rest relaxed on the knees or with the right hand on top of the left, thumbs touching at the level of the navel; (3) the elbows are slightly raised away from the rib cage; (4) the spine is lengthened; (5) the chin is slightly tucked in, which lengthens the back of the neck; (6) the mouth is closed and slightly relaxed with the tip of the tongue touching the palate; and (7). the eyes' gaze rests about eight finger-widths in front of the nose.

21. The bodhisattva vow is the Mahayana pledge to help all living beings attain enlightenment. The tantric vows are Vajrayana vows and are specific to whichever Vajrayana practice one is doing, such as reciting certain prayers or mantras every day. These are detailed in Thrangu Rinpoche's *The Tibetan Vinaya*. Namo Buddha Publications, 2001.

22. This is somewhat cultural. In the Far East, including India, Tibet, China, and Japan there are numerous stories of humans who have inadvertently disturbed the *nagas* and the protectors of a place and as a result have suffered from diseases.

Glossary of Terms

alaya consciousness (Tib. *kunzhi namshe*) According to the Chittamatra or Yogachara school this is the eighth consciousness and is often called the ground consciousness or store-house consciousness. See consciousnesses, eight.

amrita (Tib. *dutsi*) A blessed substance which can cause spiritual and physical healing.

analytical meditation In the sutra tradition one begins by listening to the teachings, or studying the dharma. Then one contemplates this dharma through analytical insight which is accomplished by placing the mind in Shamatha and focusing one-pointedly on these concepts. Finally, there is actual meditation which is free from concept.

Asanga A fourth century Indian philosopher who founded the Chittamatra (Mind-only) school, and wrote the five treatises transmitted to him by the Maitreya Bodhisattva, considered crucial within the Mahayana vehicle. His brother was the scholar Vasubhandu.

Atisha (982-1059 C.E.) Buddhist scholar at Vikramashila University, India, who came to Tibet at the invitation of King Yeshe Ö to overcome the damage done to Buddhism by the King Langdarma. With the help of his student Dromtonpa, he founded the Kadampa tradition. His most famous work is *The Lamp for the Path of Enlightenment*.

bardo means "interval." There are six kinds of bardos, but generally refers to the time between death and birth in a new body.

blessing When an individual has great devotion, he or she is able to "tap into" or receive the blessings or energy created by the Buddhas and bodhisattvas. The blessings of the lineage are always there, but can only be received if one makes oneself receptive to them, so they are not something externally bestowed by more enlightened beings.

bodhichitta Literally, the "mind of enlightenment." There are two kinds of bodhichitta: ultimate bodhichitta, which is completely awakened mind that sees the emptiness of phenomena, and relative bodhichitta, which is the aspiration to practice the six paramitas and free all beings from the suffering of samsara.

bodhisattva Literally, "one who exhibits the mind of enlightenment." Also, an individual who is committed to the Mahayana path of practicing compassion and the six paramitas in order to achieve Buddhahood and free all beings from samsara. More specifically, the term refers to those motivated to achieve liberation from samsara, who are on one of the ten bodhisattva levels, which culminate in Buddhahood.

bodhisattva vow The promise to practice in order to bring all other living beings to Buddhahood.

Bon A pre-Buddhist religion still practiced in Tibet.

Brahmin A Hindu of the highest caste who usually performs the priestly functions.

Buddha nature (Skt. *tathagatagarbha*, Tib. *deshin shekpay nyingpo*) The original nature present in all beings which, when realized, leads to enlightenment. It is also often called Buddha nature.

Buddha Shakyamuni Shakyamuni Buddha, often called Gautama Buddha, refers to the fourth and most recent Buddha of this eon, who lived sometime between 563 and 483 B.C.E.

Buddhadharma The teachings of the Buddha.

Chenrezig (Skt. *Avalokiteshvara*) Deity of boundless compassion.

Chö means "to cut off," referring to a practice that is designed to cut off all ego involvement and defilements. The practice was founded by the famous yogini, Machig Labdron (1031 to 1139 C.E.).

clarity (Tib. *selwa*) Also translated as "luminosity" or "radiant clarity." The nature of mind is that it is empty of inherent existence. But it is not just voidness, because it has clarity, which is the awareness or knowing aspect of the mind. The clarity and emptiness of mind's nature are inseparable.

compassion (Skt. *karuna*, Tib. *nyingje*) In Buddhist terms this is the impartial desire for the liberation of all living beings. This feeling can only be developed with extensive meditation and an understanding of the Buddhist path.

consciousnesses, eight These are the five sensory consciousnesses of sight, hearing, smell, taste, touch, and body sensation. The sixth consciousness is mental consciousness which does our ordinary thinking. The seventh consciousness is afflicted (klesha) consciousness which is the ever-present feeling of "I." Finally, the eighth consciousness is the ground (or alaya) consciousness which is the basis of, or holds the other consciousnesses together and also stores karmic latencies.

conventional truth (Tib. *kundzop*) There are two truths: the conventional, or relative, and the ultimate. Relative truth is how an ordinary (unenlightened) person perceives the world, with all of his or her projections based on a false belief in self.

conditioned existence (Skt. *samsara*) Ordinary existence which contains suffering because one still possesses attachment, aggression, and ignorance. Its opposite is liberation or nirvana.

dakini A yogini who has attained high realizations of the fully enlightened mind. She may be a human being who has achieved such attainments or a non-human manifestation of the enlightened mind of a meditational deity.

dharma This has two main meanings: any truth, such as that the sky is blue, or, as used in this text, the teachings of the Buddha (also called Buddhadharma).

dharmadhatu The all-encompassing, beginningless space, out of which all phenomena arise. The Sanskrit means "the essence of phenomena" and the Tibetan means "the expanse of phenomena," but usually it refers to the emptiness which is the essential nature of phenomena.

disturbing emotion (Skt. *klesha*) The emotional obscurations (in contrast to intellectual obscurations) which are also translated as "afflictions" or "poisons." The three main kleshas are passion or attachment; aggression or anger; and ignorance or delusion. The five kleshas include the three above, plus pride and envy, or jealousy.

dzo (Tib.) A cross-breed between a yak and a cow.

Dzogchen (Skt. *mahasandhi*) Also known as the "great perfection," the highest form of meditation of the nine yanas according to the Nyingma tradition. It is a meditation on examining mind directly.

four ordinary foundations or **four thoughts that turn the mind** These are the four thoughts that turn the mind. They are reflection on precious human birth, impermanence and the inevitability of death, karma and its effects, and the pervasiveness of suffering in samsara.

Gampopa (1079-1153 C.E.) One of the main holders of the Kagyu lineage in Tibet. A student of Milarepa who established the first Kagyu monastery. His best-known text is *The Jewel Ornament of Liberation*.

Geshe A scholar who has attained a doctorate in Buddhist studies. This usually takes fifteen to twenty years.

god realm See realms, six.

ground consciousness or alaya consciousness, the eighth consciousness which has the function of storing all the latent karmic imprints of experience.

hell realm See realms of samsara.

Hinayana Literally, the "lesser vehicle." This term refers to the first teachings of the Buddha which emphasized the careful examination of mind and its confusion. Also known as the Theravada, or foundational path.

hungry ghost (Skt. *preta*, Tib. *yidak*) A type of being who is always starving and thirsty as a result of excessive greed in previous lifetimes. Pretas are depicted as having enormous stomachs and thin throats. See the realms of samsara.

intermediate state See bardo.

initiation or **empowerment** (Tib. *wong*, Skt. *abhisheka*) To perform Vajrayana practice, one must receive the empowerment from a qualified lama. One should also receive the practice instruction (Tib. *tri*) and the textual reading transmission (Tib. *lung*).

Jamgon Kongtrul (1813-1899 C.E.) Also known as Lodro Thaye. He was best known for founding the Rime movement, a non-sectarian, eclectic movement which preserved various practice lineages that were on the verge of extinction. He is famous as the author of the *Five Treasures*.

jealous god See realms, six

Kadampa One of the major schools in Tibet, founded by Atisha.

Kagyu One of the four major schools of Buddhism in Tibet. It was founded by Marpa and is headed by His Holiness Karmapa. The other three are the Nyingma, Sakya, and Geluk schools.

karma Literally "action." Karma is a principle of cause and effect: when one performs a wholesome action, one's circumstances will improve, and when one performs an unwholesome action, negative results will eventually occur.

kayas, three There are three bodies, or dimensions, of the Buddha: the dharmakaya, sambhogakaya, and nirmanakaya. The dharmakaya, also called the "truth body," is the complete enlightenment, or complete wisdom of the Buddha with this realm being un-originated, beyond form, and manifests in the sambhogakaya and the nirmanakaya. The sambhogakaya, also called the "enjoyment body," manifests only to bodhisattvas on the eighth, ninth, and tenth bodhisattva levels. The nirmanakaya, known as the "emanation body," manifests in the world as a human beings such as the Shakyamuni Buddha.

kusulu There are two approaches to the spiritual path: one is to study the Buddhist texts extensively and is called the path of the scholar (pandita), and the other is to meditate directly with little study and is called the path of the kusulu (simple meditator).

lama (Skt. *guru*) A spiritual teacher.

loving-kindness (Skt. *maitri*, Tib. *jampa*) The wish that all beings have happiness.

luminosity (Tib. *selwa*) In the Buddha's third turning of the wheel of dharma everything is empty, but this emptiness is not a blank state because it is inseparable from luminosity. Luminosity, also called clarity, points to the mind's ability to know and manifest.

luminous clarity See luminosity.

Mahamudra Literally, "great seal," meaning that all phenomena are sealed by the primordially and perfectly true nature. This form of meditation is traced back to Saraha (8th century) and was passed down in the Kagyu School through Marpa. It emphasizes perceiving mind directly rather than through rationalistic analysis.

Mahayana Literally, the "great vehicle." These are the teachings of the second turning of the wheel of dharma, which emphasize emptiness, compassion, and universal Buddha nature.

Marpa Lotsawa (1012-1097 C.E.) One of the founders of the Kagyu lineage in Tibet, who made three trips to India to study and bring back tantric texts, including the Six Yogas of Naropa, the Guhyasamaja, and the Chakrasamvara practices. His teacher was Naropa, and his chief student, Milarepa.

nadi (Tib. *tsa*) Subtle channels through which the subtle energies (Skt. *vayu*) flow.

naga A water spirit which may take the form of a serpent. Nagas are often the custodians of treasures, so they keep texts or actual material treasures underground.

Naropa (1016-1100 C.E.) An Indian master who is best known for transmitting many Vajrayana teachings, in particular the Six Yogas of Naropa to Marpa, who took these back to Tibet prior to the Moslem invasion of India.

ngondro Tibetan for "preliminary practice." One usually begins the Vajrayana path by doing the four preliminary practices which involve doing 100,000 refuge prayers and prostrations, and the same number of Vajrasattva mantras, mandala offerings, and guru yoga practices.

oral instructions (Tib. *men ngak*) Sometimes called the quintessential or pith instructions. These are instructions given directly from guru to student concerning meditation and the nature of mind. While some of these are written down, many are passed on orally.

pandita A great scholar.

placement meditation As used here, there are two kinds of meditation: the analytical meditation of the pandita (or scholar), which involves conceptual analysis of phenomena, and the placement meditation of the kusulu (or simple meditator), which involves simply relaxing the mind and examining what is there without engaging in any conceptual or analytical activity.

precious nectar or **amrita** (Tib. *dutsi*) A blessed substance which can cause spiritual and physical healing.

pure realm Realms manifested by Buddhas which are totally free from suffering, and in which dharma can be received directly. These realms are presided over by various Buddhas such as Amitabha, Avalokiteshvara, and Maitreya.

realms of samsara, six These are the possible types of births for beings in samsara: the god realm, in which gods have great pride; the asura realm in which the jealous gods try to maintain what they have; the human realm which is the best realm because one has the possibility of achieving enlightenment; the animal realm characterized by stupidity; the hungry ghost realm characterized by great craving; and the hell realm characterized by aggression.

rinpoche Literally, "very precious," used as a term of respect for a Tibetan guru.

root guru A teacher from whom one has received the instructions and empowerments that form the core of one's practice.

samaya (Tib. *damtsig*) The Vajrayana vows or commitments made to a teacher or practice.

samsara Conditioned existence of ordinary life in which suffering occurs because one still possesses attachment, aggression, and ignorance. Its opposite is nirvana.

Serlingpa Dharmakirti Atisha's main teacher and source for the teachings on mind training.

Seven-Branch prayer The seven branch practice is (1) prostrating to the Three Jewels, (2) confessing negative actions, (3) making offering, (4) rejoicing in the virtue of others, (5) requesting to turn the wheel of dharma, (6) beseeching the lama not to pass into nirvana, and (7) dedicating the merit to the enlightenment of all living beings.

seven points of Vairochana These are the main positions of posture for meditation: (1) Straighten the upper body and the spinal column, (2) Look slightly downward into space straight across from the tip of the nose while keeping the chin and neck straight, (3) Straighten the shoulder blades in the manner of a vulture flexing its wings, (4) Keep the lips touching gently, (5) Let the tip of the tongue touch the upper palate, (6) Form the legs into either the lotus (Skt. *padmasana*) or the diamond (Skt. *vajrasana*) posture, and (7) Keep the back of the right hand flat on the left open palm with the inside of the tips of the thumbs gently touching.

Shamatha or **tranquility meditation** (Tib. *shinay*) A basic meditation in which, while sitting cross-legged, one follows the breath and observes the workings of the mind. The main purpose of Shamatha meditation is to settle or tame the mind so that it will stay where one places it.

sangha These are the companions on the path. The word may refer to anyone on the path, or to the noble sangha, who are realized ones.

Shantideva (675-725 C.E.) A great Bodhisattva who lived in the 7th and 8th centuries in India, and was known for his two works on bodhisattva conduct.

sending and taking practice (Tib. *tonglen*) A meditation practice promulgated by Atisha in which the practitioner takes on the negative conditions of others and gives out all that is positive.

six realms of samsara See realms of samsara.

six tastes These are sweet, sour, bitter, astringent, hot, and salty.

stupa A dome-shaped monument to the Buddha which often contains relics and remains of the Buddha or great Bodhisattvas.

subtle channels (Skt. *nadi*, Tib. *tsa*). These refer to the subtle channels through which the psychic energies or "winds" (Skt. *prana*, Tib. *lung*) travel. They correspond only loosely to the body's physical veins and arteries.

shunyata Usually translated as "emptiness." In the second turning of the wheel of dharma, the Buddha taught that external phenomena and internal phenomena, or the concept of self or "I," have no real existence and are therefore empty.

sugatagarbha (Tib. *desheg nyingpo*) "The heart of the one gone to bliss" refers to that enlightened and joyous nature present in all beings.

tantra One can divide Tibetan Buddhism into the sutra tradition and the tantra tradition. The sutra tradition primarily involves the academic study of the Mahayana sutras, while the tantric path primarily involves the practice of Vajrayana. The tantras are primarily the texts of the Vajrayana practices.

tathagatagarbha (Tib. *deshin shekpai nyingpo*) The very heart of the tathagatas, which is usually translated as Buddha nature. It is the seed or potential of enlightenment possessed by all living beings, which allows them to attain Buddhahood.

torma A ritual object made of dried barley and butter, placed on a shrine as a symbolic offering to the deities.

two truths Relative, or conventional, truth is the world as we normally experience it with seemingly solid objects; the ultimate, or absolute, truth points to the empty and luminous nature of all phenomena.

ultimate truth (Tib. *dondam*) The ultimate truth, also called absolute truth, can only be perceived by an enlightened individual is that all phenomena, both internal (thoughts and feelings) and external (the outside world) do not have any inherent existence.

Vajradhara (Tib. *Dorje Chang*) The name of the dharmakaya Buddha. Many of the teachings of the Kagyu lineage came from Vajradhara.

Vajrayana There are three major vehicles of Buddhism: Hinayana, Mahayana, and Vajrayana. The Vajrayana is based on the tantras, emphasizes the clarity aspect of phenomena, and is mainly practiced in Tibet.

Vasubhandu A great fourth-century Indian scholar, the brother of Asanga, who wrote the *Abhidharmakosha*, explaining the Abhidharma.

Vinaya These are the teachings by the Buddha concerning proper conduct, the vows, and community life.

yidam A tantric meditation deity that embodies the qualities of Buddhahood and is practiced in the Vajrayana.

Glossary of Tibetan Terms

Tibetan	Spelling in Tibetan	English
bardo	bar do	interval
Bon	bon	Bon
Chenrezig	spyan ras gzigs	Avalokiteshvara
chö	gcod	chö
dal wa gye	dal ba brgyad	eight freedoms
damtsig	dam tshig	samaya
desheg nyingpo	de gshegs snying po	Buddha nature
dondam denpa	don dam pai' bden pa	ultimate truth
Dorje Chang	rdo rje chang	Vajradhara
dutsi	bdud rtsi	amrita
dzo	mdzo	yak and cow
Dzogchen	rdzogs pa chen po	Great Perfection
geshe	dge bshes	geshe
jampa	byams pa	loving-kindness
jor wa chu	'byor ba chu	ten freedoms
Kadampa	bka' gdams pa	Kadampa
Kagyu	bka' brgyud	Kagyu
khorwa	'khor ba	samsara
kundzop	kun rdzob	relative truth
kunzhi namshe	kun gzhi' rnam shes	alaya consciousness
kunzhi yeshe	kun gzhi' ye shes	alaya wisdom
lama	bla ma	lama
lojong	blo sbyong	mind training
lung	rlung	prana
men ngak	man ngag	pith instructions
ngondro	sngon'gro	preliminary practice
nyingje	snying rje	compassion
nyon mong	nyon mongs	disturbing emotions

rinpoche	rin po che	precious one
selwa	gsal ba	luminosity
shedra	bshad grwa	monastic college
shinay	gzhi gnas	Shamatha
thangka	thang ka	scroll painting
thekpa chenpo	theg pa chen po	Mahayana
thekpa chungwa	theg pa chung ba	Hinayana
tri	'khrid	practice instructions
tonglen	gtong len	taking and sending
torma	gtor ma	torma
tsa	rtsa	subtle channels
tsaway lama	rtsa ba'i bla ma	root guru
wang	dbang	initiation
yadik	yi dvags	hungry ghost
yenlag dunpa	yan lag bdun pa	Seven-Branch prayer
yidam	yi dam	yidam

Bibliography

Allione, Tsultrim. *Women of Wisdom*. Boston: Routledge and Kegan Paul, 1984.

Dharmarakshita. *The Wheel of Sharp Weapons* (Tib. *mtshon cha'khor lo*) Dharamsala: Library of Tibetan Works and Archives, 1976.

Kyabgon, Traleg. *The Benevolent Mind: A Manual in Mind Training*. Auckland, New Zealand: Zhyisil Chokyi Ghatsal Publications, 2003.

Kongtrul, Jamgon. *The Great Path of Awakening: A Commentary on the Mahayana Teaching of the Seven Points of Mind Training*. Translated by Ken McLeod. Boston: Shambhala, 1987.

Patrul Rinpoche. *Words of My Perfect Teacher*. Translated by the Padmakara Translation Group. San Francisco: Harper-Collins Publisher, 1994.

Pel, Namkha. *Mind Training like the Rays of the Sun*. Translated by Brian Beresford. Dharamsala: Library of Tibetan Works and Archives, 1992.

Rabten, Geshe, and Geshe Dhargyey. *Advice from a Spiritual Friend*. Translated by Brian Beresford. Boston: Wisdom Publications, 1977, 1996.

Rinpoche, Dilgo Khyentse. *Enlightened Courage*. Translated by the Padmakara Translation Group. Ithaca: Snow Lion Publications, 1993.

Shantideva. *Guide to the Bodhisattva's Way of Life* (Skt. *Bodhicharyavatara*) (Tib. *byang chub sems dpa'i spyod pa la'jug pa*). The root verses translated by Marion Matric and commentary by Thrangu Rinpoche. Namo Buddha Publications, 1998.

Thrangu Rinpoche. *Four Foundations of Buddhist Practice.* Crestone: Namo Buddha Publications, 2001.

Thrangu Rinpoche. *Open Door to Emptiness.* Karme Theckchen Choling,1997.

Thrangu Rinpoche. *Transcending Ego: Distinguishing Consciousness from Wisdom.* Crestone: Namo Buddha Publications, 2001.

Thrangu Rinpoche. *The Tibetan Vinaya.* Namo Buddha Publications, 1990.

Trungpa, Chogyam. *Training the Mind and Cultivating Loving-Kindness.* Boston: Shambhala Publications, 1993.

Tulku, Gomo. *Becoming a Child of the Buddhas.* Translated by Joan Nicell. Boston: Wisdom Publications, 1998.

Wallace, B. Alan. *Buddhism with an Attitude*, Ithaca: Snow Lion Publications, 2001.

Wallace, B. *The Seven-Point Mind Training*, Ithaca: Snow Lion Publications, 1992, 2004.

Index

About the Author

THRANGU RINPOCHE WAS BORN in Kham in 1933. At the age of five he was formally recognized by the Sixteenth Karmapa and the previous Situ Rinpoche as the incarnation of the great Thrangu tulku. Entering Thrangu monastery, from the ages of seven to sixteen he studied reading, writing, grammar, poetry, and astrology, memorized ritual texts, and completed two preliminary retreats. At sixteen under the direction of Khenpo Lodro Rabsel he began the study of the three vehicles of Buddhism while staying in retreat.

At twenty-three he received full ordination from the Karmapa. When he was twenty-seven Rinpoche left Tibet for India at the time of the Chinese military takeover. He was called to Rumtek, Sikkim, where the Karmapa had his seat in exile. At thirty-five he took the geshe examination before 1500 monks at Buxador monastic refugee camp in Bengal, and was awarded the degree of Geshe Lharampa. On his return to Rumtek he was named Abbot of Rumtek monastery and the Nalanda Institute for Higher Buddhist studies at Rumtek. He has been the personal teacher of the four principal Karma Kagyu tulkus: Shamar Rinpoche, Situ Rinpoche, Jamgon Kongtrul Rinpoche, and Gyaltsab Rinpoche.

Thrangu Rinpoche has traveled extensively throughout Europe, the Far East and the USA and is the abbot of Gampo Abbey, Nova Scotia, Canada. In 1984 he spent several months in Tibet where he ordained over 100 monks and nuns and visited several monasteries. In Nepal Rinpoche has also founded a monastery, Thrangu Tashi Choling in Bodhanath, a retreat center and college at Namo Buddha, east of the Katmandu Valley, and has established a school in Bodhanath for the general education of lay children and young monks. He also has built in Katmandu Tara Abbey offering a full dharma education for nuns. He has also completed a beautiful monastery in Sarnath, India a few minutes walking distance from where the Buddha gave his first teaching on the Four Noble Truths.

Thrangu Rinpoche has given teachings in over twenty-five countries and is especially known for taking complex teachings and making them accessible to Western students. Thrangu Rinpoche is a recognized master of Mahamudra meditation.

More recently, because of his vast knowledge of the Dharma, he was appointed by His Holiness the Dalai Lama to be the personal tutor for the Seventeenth Karmapa.

Thrangu Rinpoche has centers in India, Nepal, Thailand, Malaysia, Tibet, Hong Kong, Taiwan, England, Germany, United States, and Canada. For more information on his activities, yearly teachings, and centers, please visit his website: www.rinpoche.com.

Namo Buddha Publications is dedicated to propagate the teachings of Thrangu Rinpoche and is now located at the Vajra Vidya Retreat Center in Crestone, Colorado (about four hours drive from Denver). For more information on the twenty-eight books of Thrangu Rinpoche in English visit: www.NamoBuddhaPub.org.

CARE OF DHARMA BOOKS

Dharma books contain the teachings of the Buddha. They have the power to protect against lower rebirth and to point the way to liberation. Therefore, they should be treated with respect.

These considerations may be also kept in mind for dharma artwork, as well as the written teachings and artwork of other religions.